THE 25 HOUR
WOMAN

Scripture verses identified NAS are from the New American Standard Bible, © The Lockman Foundation 1960, 1962, 1963, 1968, 1971, 1972, 1973, 1975, 1977.

Scripture verses identified TLB are taken from *The Living Bible,* copyright © 1971 by Tyndale House Publishers, Wheaton, Ill. Used by permission.

"Bionic or Bust" by Sybil Stanton, copyright © 1984 by Sybil Stanton.

Excerpt by Harriet B. Braiker, from "At Last! A New Way to Manage Stress That Really Works for Women," reprinted with permission from *Working Woman Magazine.* Copyright © 1984, HAL Publications, Inc.

Excerpts from *The Road Less Traveled,* by M. Scott Peck, M.D., copyright © 1978 by M. Scott Peck, M.D. Reprinted by permission of Simon & Schuster, Inc.

Excerpts from *Psycho-Cybernetics* by Maxwell Maltz copyright © 1960 by Prentice-Hall, Inc. Reprinted by permission of the publisher, Prentice-Hall, Inc., Englewood Cliffs, New Jersey.

Excerpts from *Feeling Good* by David D. Burns, M.D., copyright © 1980 by David D. Burns, M.D. Used by permission of William Morrow & Company.

Excerpts from *Organize Your Life* by Amy Vanderbilt. Copyright © 1966 by Nelson Doubleday, Inc.

Excerpts taken from *The Sensation of Being Somebody,* by Maurice E. Wagner. Copyright © 1975 by Maurice E. Wagner. Used by permission of Zondervan Publishing House.

Extracts from "Somewhere," by Walter de la Mare used by permission of the Literary Trustees of Walter de la Mare and The Society of Authors as their representative.

Library of Congress Cataloging in Publication Data

Stanton, Sybil.
 The 25-hour woman.

 1. Women—Conduct of life. 2. Success. 3. Women—
Religious life. I. Title. II. Title: Twenty-five-hour
woman.
BJ1610.S73 1986   158'.1'088042   86-6759
ISBN 0-8007-1487-3

To Mom,
who never keeps anyone waiting,
and to Dad,
who was always on time

_____

Contents

PART FOUR
HOW DO YOU PUT IT ALL TOGETHER?

Be his my special thanks,
Whose even-balanced soul,
From first youth tested up to
 extreme old age,
Business could not make dull,
 nor passion wild:
Who saw life steadily and saw
 it whole.

MATTHEW ARNOLD
Tribute to Sophocles

Introduction

Are You a 25-Hour Woman?

If you come to the end of the day before you reach the end of your "to do" list, this book is meant for you. If undone tasks leave you feeling frustrated, overwhelmed, inadequate, or guilty, read on.

You are a 25-Hour Woman. You are creative, conscientious, and caring. You juggle more roles than any man you know, and probably more effectively. You help others accomplish their goals, but seem never to get to your own. You put in a full and diligent day, but somehow always end up an hour short.

My understanding of the 25-Hour Woman evolved over a number of years. The process was slow, but it was accelerated by one jarring occasion I will never forget.

It was a beautiful day in the San Bernardino Mountains of Southern California, and I sat at a kitchen table with two worn-out women. I had just watched one unload twelve heaping bags of groceries from the back of her station wagon. I knew she had a husband and five active children to feed, yet I was incredulous that one week of eating required so much time and effort.

For a few peaceful moments we sipped tea together and sighed (I was worn-out, too, and I only had myself to look after).

The air of peace soon turned to one of perplexity. Mainly I listened sympathetically as my two friends aired an age-old frustration: how to get it all done in a 24-hour day. I worked with their husbands in an international nonprofit organization, where my job was national women's coordinator of one division. My responsibilities included directing the personal development of our staff women, and designing ways for the wives of our staff men to participate in our goals and objectives as their schedules allowed.

These women were two of my more than 100 "charges." I was anxious to help them, but what could I say? After all, as a single woman, I didn't have PTA, car pools, soccer practice, and other activities, ad infinitum. I did have a lot of demands on my time, however, and knew about pressure and feeling trapped. Surely, I reasoned, there must be an answer to this dilemma.

At a loss, my thoughts turned to the subject of time management and the principles that were taught throughout our organization. I had helped put together the curriculum and ventured to teach parts of it from time to time. Groping for a resolution to the giant question mark that hung in the air, I blurted out, "Have you two had time management?"

My friends recoiled and one retorted, "Yes, and if I have it one more time I'll scream!" I got the picture. Actually, it had been coming into focus for a while because, ironically, I was slowly cooking in the same kettle. I was ready to scream, too. My fancy schedules and long list of goals were doing me in. Driving home down the picturesque mountainside that day, three words seemed imbedded across my windshield: Physician, heal thyself.

Looking for a prescription, I began to scrutinize my life and informally survey other people's. As I traveled from coast to coast, my staff women freely aired their frustrations and those of their clients and protégées. They all encouraged me to return with hope for their overscheduled, underproductive days. And I did.

My quest led to a perspective on time management that has

greatly improved my life. I've passed it on through seminars to women who are in the work force and women who aren't (Yes, Virginia, there *are* full-time homemakers!), and they have gratefully reported similar changes for the better. To name just a few of my own personal triumphs:

I do less now and get more done.
I take time for *me*.
I relax without feeling guilty.
I'm better disciplined, yet more flexible.
I've stopped trying to be a superwoman.
I don't even *want* to be a superwoman anymore!

Traditional training in time management focuses on the workplace and isolates one's professional from one's personal life. Yet the more diversified our roles become, the more we need to see how they fit together. That goes for every woman, including mothers who stay in the home and singles who don't share their clock with a spouse or children. We all feel the pull from various directions and the need to fight fragmentation.

Goals and schedules offer only a partial solution. They are important, but they aren't enough. In fact, they can aggravate the frustration rather than alleviate it if not understood within a broader reference. That broader reference is concerned with the need to see the meaning of life in the mechanics of life. *To know why you are here and what it will take to satisfy you.* To value yourself enough to stop cracking the whip for the sake of keeping your wits. To enjoy, rather than endure, the process of life. This book does address the whats and whens of your life, but it gives equal time to the whys and wherefores.

Following one of my seminars, a woman wrote, "Wish all my friends could have been here." Now they can. I have adapted the same principles and presented them in these chapters. What is here is a window on my own war with time. This is not an exhaustive encyclopedia of management tools and techniques. Rather, I offer a basic philosophy backed by enough practical helps to make a difference in your life. You might call this Personal Management 101. If you have already had the advanced courses, but still spin your wheels, you may benefit from returning to the rudiments.

At the heart of management output is a management outlook. Perhaps you have never articulated yours; but if you were to give it some thought, you might recognize a negative bent that villainizes time and your management of it. You may unconsciously see time management as a necessary evil, so to speak. Such sentiment can only be self-defeating and keep you and your schedule at arm's length.

Behind every rite and ritual of effective management is a principle to embrace. Your attitude toward time management determines your success with the methods. I have tried to present both in a balanced perspective.

Someone has said, "Life is like a coin: You can spend it any way you want, but you can spend it only once." You hold the purse; your world holds the choices. Welcome to a personal shopping spree in the store of life!

PART ONE

Who Are You and Why Are You Here?

This is the true joy in life, the being used for a purpose recognized by yourself as a mighty one.

GEORGE BERNARD SHAW

Bionic or Bust

Bionic's my name.
Achieving's my fame;
I juggle 10 balls
Without any strain.

Ball 1 is the office,
Where I'm an exec;
Ball 2 is my home,
Where I keep things in check.

Ball 3 is the children,
Ball 4 is my spouse;
Ball 5 is den mother
For eight little scouts.

Ball 6 is the church,
And committees I lead;
Ball 7's the refugees
I help to feed.

Ball 8 is my hobby
Of painting still life;
Ball 9 is my parties
That everyone likes.

Ball 10 is the rest of
The things that I do—
I bake, sew and garden,
To name just a few.

There's nothing beyond me,
I'm really quite able;
And if you've not guessed it,
I'm also a fable!

1

Effectiveness:
Beyond Efficiency

W hen I was a little girl, I spent many a summer day at the playground near my home. Along with the slide, swings, and jungle gyms, we had a merry-go-round. I met my friends there, and we ran marathons to see who could last longest going round and round and round. Inevitably I got stuck for hours (or so it seemed back then). Someone always kept the wooden wheel spinning, and it was nearly impossible to get off. Of course, I wouldn't give in and yell "uncle," because I didn't want to be a sissy. So I held onto the bars for dear life and went in circles until I felt sick. I always welcomed being called home for dinner.

I don't remember ever liking those rides and was always relieved to get off. But for some reason I kept going back. At some point I either grew up and did other things or got smart and said, "I don't need this!"

Do you ever feel as though you are on the merry-go-round of life? You go in circles until you're drained and dizzy but don't have enough sense to stop. You hate every minute of it but keep going back for more; you've even prided yourself at lasting longer than your friends. Secretly, though, you wish someone would blow the whistle, stop the ride, and let you off.

You will never be able to stop the clock, but you *can* put a

halt to whirling around wearisomely and, worse, getting nowhere. There will always be merry-go-rounds, but you don't
have to be on one.

If you are accustomed to doing everything in a flurry, you
may find it difficult to change your modus operandi. Likely,
you're convinced that it's necessary, and you've probably even
learned to impress people with your busyness.

The late historian Will Durant said, "No one who is in a
hurry is quite civilized." I remember the day I thought something was wrong because I wasn't rushing, and I wondered if I
were losing drive, because I felt no panic. Yet I had accomplished a lot, I wasn't behind schedule, and I had time to spare.
Then I realized what was happening: I was becoming civilized.

In her classic best-seller *Gift From the Sea,* Anne Morrow
Lindbergh spoke of battling the frustration of functioning in
the twentieth century:

> Life today in America is based on the premise of
> ever-widening circles of contact and communication. It
> involves not only family demands, but community de-
> mands, national demands. . . . my mind reels with it.
> What a circus act we women perform every day of our
> lives. It puts the trapeze artist to shame. . . . This is not
> the life of simplicity but the life of multiplicity that the
> wise men warn us of. . . . Woman's life today is tending
> more and more toward the state William James de-
> scribes so well in the German word "Zerrissenheit—
> torn-to-pieces-hood."[1]

Mrs. Lindbergh went on to say, in essence, that we cannot
ignore the problem and hope it goes away. Neither can we let it
get the best of us. We need to find a balance somewhere. That
balance, she concluded, lies in "cultivating techniques of living."

My goal for this book is to help you cultivate a technique of
living—called effectiveness. For the first thirty years of my life,
however, I cultivated another technique—efficiency.

I have always thrived on order. As far back as I can remember, few personal projects or possessions escaped my organizational enterprise. I systematized, standardized, routinized, and methodized everything in my room.

I even had a system for sorting all the candy I hauled in on Halloween ... and I hauled it in! My brothers and I took trick-or-treating seriously, and mapped out a strategy to get the most for our mileage. We learned the houses and neighborhoods that netted the biggest and best treats, and we headed decisively in those directions. On Halloween night we returned home at least once to unload our bags and go out again. We collected so much stuff that I put my share in shoeboxes by category—one for bubble gum, one for candy bars, one for Tootsie Rolls, and so forth. One year I had so many lollipops, I had separate boxes for each flavor!

My organizational skills grew more sophisticated over the years, and eventually qualified me for good jobs during high school, college, and after. At work, not only did I always do more than my job called for, I also piled on church and community work. But one day in my early thirties, I verged on burnout, if not breakdown. I saw an article titled, "Our Way of Life May Be Killing Us," and I knew mine was. Organization wasn't the answer, because I couldn't *get* any more organized. Where was the solution to be found?

Efficiency or Effectiveness?

First, I had to figure out the problem. In my solemn search I made a startling discovery: I had majored in efficiency at the cost of effectiveness. Organization had become an end in itself rather than a means to an end. *Efficiency, I heard someone explain, is doing things right; effectiveness is doing the right things.* Efficiency is vital to time management, but never at the cost of effectiveness.

The difference between efficiency and effectiveness is the difference between organization and management. The dictionary offers some insight here. To *organize* means "to systematize; to give structure to." To *manage* means "to bring about; to succeed in accomplishing a task or purpose." Organization attends to the "parts," while management gives mind to the "whole." Management is the pie, organization is the pieces. Organization without management is an island of excellence in a sea of confusion.

Picture your dream-house kitchen, and imagine it fully equipped and immaculately intact. That's organization. Now picture yourself as a gracious hostess employing your kitchen and cookbooks to serve a beautiful five-course meal. That's management!

Though I was well organized for many years, I was not well managed. I generally succeeded in accomplishing my tasks and purposes, but not without nearly having a nervous breakdown in the process! My mother used to say, "I bet that on the day you get married, you'll be running to the store for a new pair of nylons an hour before the wedding!"

Today I still thrive on order, but now it is the cart *behind* the horse. Organization must always serve a purpose, not thwart it. Too often schedules and structure frustrate a person's desires, when they should help fulfill them.

Common Fears About Time Management

Countless women confess to me their reservations and suspicions concerning time management. One that is consistently voiced is the fear of inflexibility. People envision themselves turning into rigid robots, complying with strict demands. They fear losing spunk and spontaneity. When they see me coming, they stiffen their posture and straighten everything in sight. Unfortunately many people, in the name of management, promote that impression and convey such expectations. Hardly a model worth following.

An effectively managed woman, by contrast, moves from one activity to another with ease and a kind of rhythm. She exudes graciousness and certainly never flaunts her schedule. She is in control, but you don't read it all over her face. She can run a tight ship and still reflect a serene spirit. You can, too. Why manage your time if it turns you into an ogre? Nobody needs that! I'm often tempted to make my first appearance to time-management audiences with a placard that reads RELAX! Because that's what an effective time manager does.

Management isn't something you do *to* yourself; it's what you do *for* yourself. I met with a group of women one month after they attended one of my seminars. Since I always emphasize that management is a process, that it takes *time,* I was skeptical when one mother of teenagers said her whole life had changed. But she displayed a new tranquillity and glow, so I asked her to elaborate. She said, simply, "I'm having fun now. Before the seminar I didn't know that fun was missing in my life. Now I get the important things done, and have plenty of time left for me." She added that a frazzled friend called her to bemoan her demanding schedule, then suddenly asked, "Why do you have time to listen to me?"

Management is also something you do for others. If you are well managed, you will impart calm to people in your path rather than impose law and order on them. A woman told me, "For the first time, when I left your seminar, I was relaxed and didn't feel that I had to get everything done. And I stopped nagging my husband to do things . . . He even commented that I was different, and now he comes to me and *asks* what he can do!"

If you major in efficiency, you won't see past your cluttered den and messy drawers. Worse, you will figuratively go crazy and take everyone with you. If you major in effectiveness, your serenity will renew you and rub off on those around you.

A common feeling about time management is the fear of having to conform to a prescribed pattern. One example is still vivid in my mind after several years. I was teaching a seminar for a church group at a weekend retreat. During the morning coffee break on the second day, a young mother pulled me aside and prepared me for some true confessions. This was her first breather since her eighteen-month-old baby was born. Her husband encouraged her to attend with her friends, and she jumped at the chance to get away. She looked forward to walking in the woods, taking time to think, and perhaps even reading a book. But she had no intention of listening to me. She voiced her view to a friend on their way to the retreat: "No woman, let alone a single one, is going to tell me to have my dishes done by eight in the morning."

But she had decided to give me the benefit of the doubt and come to one talk before making herself scarce and leaving the group. What she heard, ". . . changed my life! I realized that you did not want to put me into a mold. But more than that, I realized that God didn't either. I saw that I had lost myself in my husband and baby and had ceased to be my own person. Now I am so motivated to better manage my time and be all that I can be."

The most important ingredient of time management is you— *who you are, how you operate, what you want out of life.* These pages suggest tools and techniques to help you be a better manager. But they won't put a plan in your hands. I could give you a list of goals and a schedule of activities, but they wouldn't be yours. Only you can determine what you will do, and when and how you will do it.

I hope you never lose a sense of freedom about managing your time and life. But, remember, the other side of freedom is responsibility. The buck stops with you. A management consultant observes, "I so often hear, 'I wish I knew how to manage my time better.' Rarely do I hear, 'I wish I knew how to manage myself better.' " International management expert Alec Mackenzie says, "At the heart of time management is management of self."[2] The ball is in your court.

Still another fear the thought of managing oneself evokes is the task of taking on too much. One woman told me she stayed away from time-management seminars because, "I just can't put one more project in my garage." Her notion is a common one—that the purpose of time management is to stuff your schedule and squeeze as much as you can into a day. But the opposite is more true. I tell women at the outset of a seminar that they will more likely leave with a list of things to cancel.

The Bible urges, "Be careful how you walk, not as unwise

men, but as wise, making the most of your time. . . ."[3] We tend to translate that to say *"doing the most* with your time." But the principle here is equivalent to the modern maxim of "Work smarter, not harder." It's not how much you do, but what you accomplish, and how you go about accomplishing it, that counts.

I have a strong hunch that when we meet our Maker, we will breathlessly parade our noble activities, and He might well burst our busy bubble with a simple comment: "Hmmm, I never expected you to do all that." Learning the principles of time management just may free you from what one writer calls "the claustrophobia of compunction," and significantly shorten your list of things to do.

As a seminar instructor, few things encourage me more than eager conferees. But some arrive with such enthusiasm that I almost have to squelch their expectations. They are victims of our "instant age." You know the syndrome—the no-diet diet, the fast formula to a fantastic face, the quick cure for colds. These women come to a seminar anticipating a management makeover. They would swallow a pill for their beat-the-clock blues if I offered them one. Though I don't want to dampen their spirits, I have to remind them that there is no panacea here—just a prescription to follow for the long haul.

A writer passed the following indictment on our society: "One wit has said that the two burning questions most occupying Americans today are 'How can I lose weight?' and 'Where can I park my car?' A general spirit of superficiality encourages the majority to look for instant solutions with minimal commitment."[4]

A Need for Commitment

The technique of effective living calls for commitment. We can keep hoping for easy answers, yet deep down we all know life doesn't work that way. In my mid-twenties I decided to begin a regular home exercise program. Many were available, but I finally chose the one that promised hard work. Why? Not because I like to sweat and strain, but because I knew the author was being honest with me and offered no false hopes. She wrote in the foreword, "There is no use kidding yourself or hoping for miracles; conditioning, and keeping in condition, requires time."

While personal management doesn't come without time and effort, you will be encouraged to know that much of it does become second nature with practice. And the principles readily adapt to fluctuations in your life. The laws of management are as universal as the law of gravity—they work wherever you are, whatever your situation.

Thus far I have cited examples of married women. But single women are no less trapped on treadmills. They, too, sacrifice effectiveness because they've been sold a bill of goods that says they have to get it all in while they're "free." The problem is compounded when they want to say no to doing too much and are met with raised eyebrows because "You don't have a husband and kids, so you have a lot of time."

One load I feel particularly compassionate about is that carried by the single mother. I can imagine her pressures and problems sometimes seem insurmountable. But I have to believe that it is just as possible for her to live some kind of orderly life. My belief is supported by the very women who face this situation. Often at a seminar, a single mother will voice the impossibility of managing her time and, especially, of doing anything for herself. And every time, while I respond by acknowledging how hard it must be for her, another woman with the same circumstances will counter by saying that she has made the principles of time management work. As one single mother of four concluded, "You not only *can* do it, but you *must* if you want to stay sane."

Every stage and marital state in life has its benefits and drawbacks, *and* its time limitations. If we think the grass is greener in someone else's yard, we are mistaken. Single or married, parent or childless, with domestic help or doing it ourselves, we all face pressures. I'm sure we would alleviate some of the strain if we could appreciate one another's load rather than minimize it.

The Need to Take Stock

Some time ago I came across a cartoon that painted a more pathetic than amusing picture. A drained and disheveled woman had opened her front door to the knock of a national pollster. Three kids huddled under her elbow. She held a broom on one side and a wiggling baby on the other.

The unsuspecting pollster leaned forward, pen and pad in hand, ready to fire the questions. Before he had a chance, the overspent mom frowned, "I haven't had time to have an opinion for seven years!"

How long has it been since you expressed, or even had, a personal opinion? When was the last time you took a break to think, I mean really think?

Living effectively evolves from within. Reflection and meditation are vital, but are too often upstaged by remnants on the "to do" list. I wonder if we have lost the art of thinking and have settled for mere functioning.

One of my conferees confessed to the others, "I think I keep busy so I don't *have* to think." The others agreed and added that it was easier to keep going than to stop long enough to take serious stock of their direction.

Do you want to cultivate the technique of effective living? Then you must develop the habit of earnest listening. You cannot effectively manage the things around you until you nurture the thoughts within you.

Learning what makes you tick influences every aspect of how you manage your time and live your life. Therefore, we will keep coming back to it. If all you receive from this book is a higher regard for yourself, you will automatically treat time more effectively.

My kindergarten teacher used to say, "Put on your thinking cap." At the risk of insulting your intelligence, I'm tempted to suggest the same as you tackle this task of living. If you need a refreshing break to become reacquainted with yourself, determine to set aside a block of time to be alone. Take a walk, go out for coffee, get away to an undistracted place. If you have children, hire a baby-sitter. No price is too great for restoration.

So an exhausted mother of five children found out; and she wrote to Ann Landers about it. One Friday afternoon she met her husband at the door with her suitcase in hand and, though he "didn't understand," assured him that a motel room would be less expensive than doctor bills. She spent twenty-one hours ALONE—getting "rest and privacy you can't get at home."

Please don't abandon your children and leave your husband, because I don't want to receive a thousand angry letters from deserted families, or feel responsible for broken homes. I've simply recounted one 25-hour woman's sense of frustration and her solution, showing that where there's a will there's a way.

When you take your time of reflection, ask yourself the following questions (you will get even more out of your thoughts if you write them down):

1. What do I want out of life?
2. What, if anything, is keeping me from realizing what I want?
3. How am I helping or hindering my own fulfillment?

Justice Oliver Wendell Holmes said that while "thinking can be dull, it also can be a glorious and exciting adventure." If you are unaccustomed to contemplation, it won't come naturally or quickly, but it *will* come. It is never easy, even for monastics whose lifework is meditation. But it *is* possible to develop the art and the discipline. The reward in personal growth and depth is well worth it.

2

Self-Image:
How It Affects
Productivity

When I was in graduate school in Ann Arbor, Michigan, I arranged my schedule so I could substitute teach two days a week. It provided extra income—not to mention good experience.

One morning I was looking over the lesson plans when suddenly I felt I was being watched. Stalked, actually. The first graders had begun to come in, and one pixieish blonde was inching her way around my desk, giving me the once-over. I looked up and smiled at her.

"Are you a mommy?" she inquired.

"No," I answered, "I'm not a mommy."

"Are you a wife?"

"No, I'm not a wife either."

With that she became frustrated, and blurted out, "Well, what *are* you?"

It's the question of the ages: What, or who, am I? How would you answer that? Your response is what is known as a self-image—a mental picture you have of yourself.

When it comes to managing your life, probably nothing helps or hinders you more than your self-image. Remember the saying "What you see is what you get"? There's a lot of practical truth in that. You can't produce more than you can perceive.

"For as he thinketh in his heart, so is he." Psychologist and author Cecil Osborne paraphrases this verse from Proverbs 23:7 in *The Art of Understanding Yourself*: "Whatever you feel yourself to be at the center of your emotional nature, that is what you really are, existentially, and *your actions will be in harmony with your self-concept*" (emphasis mine).[1] Do you see how this relates to effectiveness? You may have great goals and super schedules, but they will be continually frustrated if you lack the confidence to carry them out. You may have all the potential in the world, but unless you really believe in yourself, it is basically useless to you . . . or anyone else.

When I was discussing this with a woman in one of my seminars, she nodded knowingly and related the following story, which illustrates this point.

"I was paired in a work situation with a gifted woman. Our strengths complemented each other's, and I envisioned our being a dynamic duo. But after nearly twelve months together, we had spun our wheels more than we made mileage. Though I had many glimpses of all she was capable of, I saw few complete pictures of actual results. She prided herself on her abilities, but she seldom applied all or any of them wholeheartedly. It seemed the more I encouraged her, the less she produced. Worse, while she boasted of her expertise, she belittled others' efforts. I believed in her and freely communicated that I did. So did others. But she didn't believe in herself. Sadly, I expended more energy pampering her sensitive spirit than pursuing our given tasks. Neither of us batted a thousand that year."

Have you ever considered how much your self-image determines your outlook and output? Psychologist Maurice Wagner sums it up this way:

> An adequate self-concept is a precious possession. It is the premise upon which a person can devote himself wholeheartedly to living a useful and productive life. It

prepares the mind to think clearly so that a person can be at his best, enables him to concentrate upon definite goals, and motivates him to a complete commitment to the task at hand.

An inadequate self-concept is a handicap. It affords no premise upon which a person can give himself completely to what he wants to do. It provides no cohesive for the various forces of the mind so that an inner wholeness can be realized, and it binds a person under the tyranny of having to measure up in some way in order to feel accepted.

Persons with an inadequate self-concept spend much attention, time, and energy trying to establish a secure premise of self-identity in each situation instead of being able to function because they already have such a premise. Some people are so completely preoccupied with feelings of being a nobody, in a world of people who seem to them to be more or less stable somebodies, that they can scarcely apply themselves to any certain task. Anxiety over possible failures and rejections and humiliations allows them no place to rest from their labors or to take pleasure from their efforts and accomplishments or to build an abiding confidence in the goodness of life.[2]

Robert Schuller, pastor of the Crystal Cathedral and TV's "Hour of Power," commissioned the Gallup organization to conduct a poll on self-esteem in America. He concluded in his book *Self-Esteem: The New Reformation* that "self-esteem . . . is the greatest need facing the human race today."[3] The poll found that 37 percent of Americans have high self-esteem, 30 percent have low self-esteem, and the remainder are those whose self-esteem is just about average.

Actually, Dr. Schuller's findings may be conservative. Some years ago, in his best-seller, *Psycho-Cybernetics,* physician Maxwell Maltz estimated that 95 percent of all people in our society feel inferior.[4] Whatever the actual statistics, a negative self-image seems to be a widespread national disorder.

How interesting that the cry today is for more time to do more things, when what we probably all need is more self-assurance that we are doing the *right* things with the time we have. How do you get that assurance? First, it helps to understand how you got where you are.

How Your Self-Image Is Formulated

Self-esteem, or lack of it, is a cumulative process. From the day you greet the world you begin to formulate your self-image. Your internal computer constantly programs external stimuli and feeds you positive or negative attitudes about yourself. That stimuli consists of all kinds of circumstances and a lot of different people.

You may be unaware of how specific persons or events have influenced you. Or you may vividly remember a particular parent, friend, neighbor, or teacher who left an indelible mark on your psyche.

A seminary professor tells of the incorrigible reputation he earned in grade school. Then he entered the sixth grade. His new teacher looked him straight in the eye and said, "Oh, *you're* Howard Hendricks. I've heard a lot about you . . . but I don't believe a word of it." Dr. Hendricks points to that time as a major turning point in his life. He says, "I met the first person in my life who ever communicated to me that they believed in me. And I never let her down."

His experience illustrates what is known as the "self-fulfilling prophecy." A self-fulfilling prophecy is the tendency for one person's expectations of another person to actually result in behavior consistent with those expectancies.[5] In other words, one's assumptions about another—positive or negative—wield such power as to actually turn into predictions.

The self-fulfilling prophecy is not just an *inter*personal dynamic, but an *intra*personal one as well. That is, not only can the expectations of one person affect the performance of another, but one's own expectancies of oneself are also predictors of success or failure. You will become what you believe. A social psychologist writes:

> I have repeatedly been struck by the fact that goals people both desire and have the ability to achieve are often relinquished, abandoned without a real effort to attain them. On the other hand, people who appear to have no more, or even less, ability, often achieve those very goals. How could this be accounted for? The answer, or so it seemed to me, was that those who relinquished their goals somehow became convinced that they could not achieve them and, hence, did not try as hard as they might have had they had a greater faith in the efficaciousness of their efforts.[6]

You are a self-fulfilled prophecy. You are what you have believed and what others have believed about you. If you are in that 37 percent of people with high self-esteem, you are very fortunate—and probably living quite effectively. But if you are in the majority, with average or low self-esteem, you would do well to assess your assumptions before you take one more step in the time-management process.

I am not a professional counselor, so I have approached this subject with considerable caution. Further, I am all too aware that bookstores abound with expert works on self-esteem. But I would be more than remiss to expound on personal management without addressing this essential issue. To do so would be to build a house without a foundation. Comments I receive from conferees after my seminars continue to confirm my conviction that effectiveness is a greater need than efficiency, and self-esteem is a major factor:

"For the first time . . . I feel this is workable because it made me realize I can work with my strengths and that I don't have to feel inferior if I fail."

"My failures in time management may be due to my terrible self-image. I now know where to start . . . and maybe even I will someday be able to manage my time."

"The most important thing I learned was that I count! . . . I didn't think I was important. . . ."

The purpose of this chapter is to make you aware of the importance of your self-image, not to overhaul the one you have. I wish I could inject everyone with a time-release shot of self-esteem, but I can't. I can, however, provide a little perspective to guide your thinking. For the remainder of the chapter we will look at some of the dynamics that reinforce a positive or negative self-image and thus facilitate or frustrate effective living. Your self-image may be healthy enough that all you need during times of normal fluctuation is a reminder or two. Our discussion may help to get you out of a slouch or over a hump when you begin to entertain self-doubts.

However, if you continually struggle with low self-esteem, you may require more than reminders. You may need reprogramming. And we can't accomplish that in these brief pages. If your conditioned reflexes consistently generate more self-rejection than acceptance, I urge you to seek sound professional help so you won't be stuck the rest of your life. A little exploration may give you a lot of relief.

Formulating a More Productive Self-Image

Remember Snow White's wicked stepmother? She got a daily dose of self-esteem from her talking mirror. "Who's fairest of us all?" she would ask as she gazed at herself. "Queen, thou art the fairest of us all," her mirror faithfully answered. Of course, the queen was never satisfied, and she returned every morning for reassurance. She was thoroughly shattered on that fateful day when the mirror announced that Snow White had blossomed into the fairest beauty in the land.

If your mirror could speak, what would you ask it? What do you need to hear to feel good about yourself?

The person you see yourself to be, while influenced initially by your unique background, is perpetuated day by day by your self-beliefs. If your belief system is out of whack, your self-image will be too.

Like Snow White's stepmother, most of us have a "mirror"

we check in with regularly. It may be a friend, a family member, a colleague, a magazine, the society page, a soap opera, the Dow Jones averages. Consciously or unconsciously, we look for our reflection in one or more sources.

These mirrors feed what psychologist Maurice Wagner cites as three fundamental concerns we have about ourselves in various life situations: our appearance, our performance, and our status. These concerns translate into questions:

Appearance: *How do I look?*
Performance: *How am I doing?*
Status: *How important am I?*[7]

Our concerns cause us to alter our appearance or strive for success or clamor for financial gain. There is nothing inherently wrong in excelling in any or all of these categories if doing so comes out of and contributes to your effectiveness. But when they become the *basis* for your self-image, you have a problem. As in the stock market, your averages are unstable. They fluctuate with the events of the day and change with the passing of time. You can't depend on the points you have this morning, because their value tonight is unpredictable. If a mirror offers any security, it is at most temporary and unreliable.

An Ann Landers column once printed a letter from a teenager who complained of having "a very big, ugly, repulsive-looking nose." She added that her nose made her "completely miserable" as well as lonely and hopeless. It was ruining her life. Ann sided with her desire to have plastic surgery, but added, "Be aware it may NOT change the way you feel about yourself."

Ann gave a wise response. She knew the young girl's self-image could not be secured by a scalpel. While a new nose might momentarily appease her depression, it might not alleviate her deeper feelings of despair.

It was this very phenomenon that led Maxwell Maltz to explore the field of psycho-cybernetics. In his practice as a plastic surgeon, he observed that "in *most cases* a person who had a conspicuously ugly face, or some 'freakish' feature corrected by surgery, experiences an almost immediate . . . rise in self-esteem, self-confidence. But in *some cases,* the patient continued to feel inadequate and experienced feelings of inferiority. In short, these 'failures' continued to feel, act and behave *just as if* they still have an ugly face. . . . [they] acquired new faces but went right on wearing the same old personality."[8] These "apparent discrepancies," he concluded, had one common denominator: the self-image.

Dr. Wagner's work validates Maltz's observation and sheds further light on this dynamic. The three concerns he identified—appearance, performance, and status—are actually surface expressions of deeper needs. At the very core of our emotional being, he explains, are "three feelings (that) integrate to form the essential elements of self-concept. They not only constitute the mental structure of self-concept, but give it support and stability. This triad of feelings is *belongingness, worthiness,* and *competence."*[9] Their interrelatedness sometimes blurs their distinctness; but it is not so important that we isolate these issues, as that we understand their interplay in our sense of worth.

> Belongingness is an awareness of being wanted and accepted, of being cared for and enjoyed. It is the "part of," or "we," feeling experienced when we sense we are wanted or desired by some person or a group of people. . . .
> Worthiness is a feeling of "I am good" or "I count" or "I am right." We feel worthy when we do as we should. We verify that sense of worthiness when we sense others' positive attitudes toward us and their hearty endorsement of our actions. . . .
> Competence is a feeling of adequacy, of courage, or hopefulness, of strength enough to carry out the tasks of daily life situations. It is the "I can" feelings of being able to face life and cope with its complexities. . . .[10]

When our feelers reach out for affirmation, what we are looking for is this sense of acceptance, worth, and adequacy.

We want to know we are okay. The problem with looking into a mirror is that sometimes we are okay, and sometimes we aren't. Even if we have gotten beyond the physical and material features and value deeper qualities, our mirror will still do us in.

A close friend wrote to tell me that the man she had been in love with for so many years called her with the news that he was marrying someone else. He even elaborated at length on the virtues of his fiancée. My friend told me, "By the time the conversation ended, I felt as though I'd just received a phone call from all the men in the world, saying I was unlovely and unwonderful and unwanted." Having "been there" myself, I felt her pain in the very pit of my stomach.

What are we to do about rebuffs and rejections? Do we have to die inside every time someone or something shatters our ego? Or can we deflect these assaults and stay intact? Do we have to disintegrate when we're discounted; or can we come out of it whole and maintain our self-respect? I think we can. My friend did, and others do—because they know who they really are.

"It is never who *You* are that hangs you up," writes marriage and family counselor Dorothy Briggs, "but rather who you *think* you are. Be aware that your self-image is learned; your Real Self is a given. To discover your Real Self, it is important to separate the Real You from your self-image. . . . Once your Self Belief System is accurate you are free of the trap of low self-esteem. You are free to be the Real You."[11]

You can program yourself with the "I'm o.k., You're o.k." philosophy; but unless it is accurate, you won't feel okay for long. You can pep up your perspective with positive-thinking seminars; but it won't stick unless your assumptions are also *proper*. I'm all for positive thinking, but not at the expense of proper thinking. And proper, or accurate, thinking holds the key to lasting self-esteem.

We seem to have revived the appeal in the old song to "accentuate the positive, eliminate the negative." While proper thinking *does* accentuate the positive, it also acknowledges the negative and sees it in the right perspective. The person who thinks properly will likewise think positively. But the positive thinker may not always be a proper thinker.

We have all known the parent whose child can do no wrong; the woman who ignores a cancerous growth; the man who denies the inevitable reality of death and leaves no will for his family; the Pollyanna who sees only the sunshine, despite the fact that you are dripping wet from a downpour. Improper thinking keeps us from confronting real issues and dealing with them constructively.

America's beloved beagle Snoopy illustrated the principle of proper thinking in one of his comic-strip appearances. As he lay atop his wooden house, deep in thought, his master, Charlie Brown, ran up to him waving a newspaper ad in the air, and saying, "It says here that they're having a dog show . . . Have you ever thought of entering a dog show?"

As Snoopy pondered the invitation, his countenance turned to puzzlement. Finally he dismissed the idea, saying, "How could I? I don't even *own* a dog."*

You might say that Snoopy has a very positive self-image. True, but it isn't a proper one. Though Snoopy is generally convinced that he qualifies for the human race, the truth remains—he is a dog.

It has been said that we should not see ourselves as worse than we are, or better than we are—but, just as we are.

Acknowledging You Inner Critic

We see ourselves just as we are when we have an *Accurate* Self-Belief System. Unfortunately, most of us also have an *Acquired* Self-Belief System that runs interference and distorts our vision. What we must separate in this acquired system are the accusations from the affirmations.

Inside your head is an "inner critic"—a judgmental voice— that is quick to put you down. It talks in a self-reproaching tone, and it tells you you're no good. It belittles, minimizes, accuses, condemns. It attacks you in generalities and says things like "I'm a terrible housekeeper," "I can't do anything

* © 1969 United Feature Syndicate, Inc.

right," "I always say the wrong thing," "I'll never get organized." Your inner critic destroys your feelings of belongingness, worthiness, and competence. And it kills any hope of being effective. In fact, it may make you drive yourself more toward overefficiency in an attempt to make yourself look and feel good.

This critic has been building a case against you for many years and has gathered grievances from many sources. Everyone who has had any kind of relationship to you has brought to that relationship his or her own inner critic and has passed on its effects.

None of us has a perfect background. Whether by commission or omission, even those who have loved us have hurt us. We are hurt by people because they've been hurt by others. They give what they can to us based on what was given to them. They can't give what they don't have. They do their best. The very fact that most of us are functioning, and functioning fairly well, means that someone did something right along the way. Nonetheless, that does not diminish or discount the hurts and injustices we have met with. And we do have a responsibility to deal with them now.

Speaking to the particular role our parents played, clinical psychologist Sonya Friedman writes, "There will come a time when you must acknowledge that your parents will never be the people you hoped they would be. When you accept that, you will be on your way to greater wisdom and emotional health. In reality, you don't have to go back and master the past through the present. . . . If you understand and accept your parents for who they are, and yourself for who you are, your only obligation is to say to them, in effect, 'Thanks, I'll take it from here.' "[12]

When I read that, I imagined myself standing at a crossroad with everyone who has ever influenced me for good or bad or both. Collectively they held out a torch, and I at once had to make a decision. I pictured myself standing erect and confident and saying, "Thanks, I'll take it from here."

Sometimes we leave people behind, but we take their accusing voices with us. Even though we are free from them physically, we are still enslaved to them emotionally. Taking the torch means leaving the "old tapes" behind. It means we silence the old recordings and make a new record. It means being "free of an inappropriate and worn-out Belief System."[13]

Affirming Your Self-Esteem

An appropriate belief system is brought about by replacing the inner critic with an inner affirmer. The affirmer squelches the critic with clear and constructive statements. It says things like "I'm a loyal friend," "I did a good job on that project," "I needed that rest," "I planned a good party." It speaks kindly to faults and failures rather than writing you off the face of the earth. It isolates your behavior from your whole being. It may tell you that you made a mistake, but it won't term you a total failure. It may even require that you make some changes; but it presents them desirably.

Instead of "I'll never learn to play tennis," the affirming voice says, "I want to improve my game," or "I'd prefer to find another sport." It counters "I'm a bad mother" with "I make good meals for my family," "I laugh a lot with my children," "I want to learn to listen better to my teenager." The affirmer builds your sense of belongingness, worthiness, and competence.

Dorothy Briggs writes:

> Each of us identifies with whatever qualities we learn to place after the words "I am." We then see such traits as "truths" about ourselves. These "truths" or self-beliefs literally screen out any messages to the contrary.
>
> You cannot hold onto a negative self-image if you let in evidence of your positives. Then to keep the identity you have built, you are driven to behave accordingly. Only in this way can you feel all of one piece—consistent internally. You live up to your programmed or conditioned self-image.[14]

Much is said these days about re-parenting or self-parenting. What it boils down to is that you give to yourself what others could not give you emotionally. You arrive at new positives to put after the words "I am." I won't give you a list of traits and talents to choose from, because that would take the torch away from you. *You* must arrive at those statements that affirm your self-esteem—those qualities you know to be inherently true or possible about yourself, that you want to begin to believe. Start by recalling instances and individuals in your past, and present, that have contributed to your self-worth. What was communicated or reinforced that caused you to hold your head higher?

If yours was a bitter background, one that offered little positive reinforcement, you may need help separating the real you from your self-image. I turn again to Dr. Friedman for practical advice:

> Your biological parents may not have given you a good model with which to identify, nor provided you with a basis for developing self-esteem. Part of re-parenting yourself out of a negative mold and into a positive one is to find a *psychological* parent—a person you hold in esteem, whose example you would like to follow. The psychological parent will function much like a mentor and will play the part of the good parent. The point is to establish some emotional connection to that person whose humanity, courage, or positive outlook will both inspire and influence you. . . . The psychological parent need not know that he or she has been chosen for this role—or even that you exist. What matters is how you interact with that person . . . or how you think you would interact if that person were a part of your life.[15]

The important thing to remember in re-parenting is not to try to reprogram people other than yourself. Don't keep looking to those who were unable to build you up in the past, to begin doing so now. This is especially hard with people you love and want to "connect" with. You keep hoping that as you change, they will come along. But what will more likely happen is that your inner critic will just be reinforced by their inability to validate you. Continue to care for those individuals, and communicate as best you can, but look to others to contribute to your list of "I ams."

Self-Esteem Is Available From God

While new and positive relationships can help a lot toward changing your self-belief system, you have probably recognized a potential weakness in this way of going about it. It is still looking to mirrors. Recognizing the problem, Dr. Maltz writes:

> How can you know the truth about yourself? How can you make a true evaluation? It seems to me that here psychology must turn to religion. The Scriptures tell us that . . . God created man in his own image. If we really believe in an all-wise, all-powerful, all-loving Creator, then we are in a position to draw some logical conclusions about that which he has created—Man. In the first place such an all-wise and all-powerful Creator would not turn out inferior products, any more than a master painter would paint inferior canvases. Such a Creator would not deliberately engineer his product to fail, any more than a manufacturer would deliberately build failure into an automobile. . . . What brings more glory, pride, and satisfaction to a father than seeing his offspring do well, succeed and express to the full their abilities and talents? . . . I cannot believe that it brings any "glory" to God when his children go around with hangdog expressions, being miserable, afraid to lift up their heads and "be somebody."[16]

I heard a minister say, "When you start your day with your mirror instead of your Maker, you'll have paralysis." Why? Because your Maker affirms your value as a person, and your mirror frustrates it. I do believe God puts people in our lives who love and accept us, and are to some extent His emissaries of encouragement. They help build our self-esteem; but they can't give or maintain it. Even our affirmers may someday let us down. Ultimately, self-esteem must come from within. Dr. Wagner expressed it in this equation: God + Me = a Whole Person.

The late Rabbi Joshua Loth Liebman, professor and popular radio speaker, wrote, "Men who are inwardly tormented and emotionally unhappy can never be good partners of God; the great ideals of religion will remain unimplemented and unfulfilled so long as unhappy, distorted men and women continue to be defective transmitters of the Divine."[17]

The "put down" voices you hear aren't from God; they are from other people, but you may have projected them onto God. Part of reprogramming your tapes is letting God re-parent you—believing He is for you.

God offers self-esteem to everyone, but He can't force it on you. You have to come to the place where you can embrace His validation for yourself. C. S. Lewis wrote, "You must have a capacity to receive, or even omnipotence can't give."[18]

Self-Esteem Is a Decision

The reverse is also true. You don't have to succumb to the pressures or attacks of your mirror. The late Eleanor Roosevelt said, "No one can make you feel inferior without your consent." Self-esteem is a decision. You are what you are today because of the choices you are making. That is not to say it is simple; but it is attainable. And only if you look in the proper place.

The ancient Greek poet Pindar said, "Become what you are." What you are is someone who is unconditionally accepted by your Maker, worthy of others' respect, and fully adequate to live a productive and satisfying life. You are wanted, you are valuable, you are able.

According to Dr. William Appleton, clinical professor of psychiatry at Harvard Medical School, "A fully realized adult woman does not depend on others for her self-esteem. In fact, she expects others to *perceive* her value, not to *create* it. She does not desire approval indiscriminately or for its own sake, but only if it is expressed because of attributes she respects in herself."[19]

In his book *How People Change,* Allen Wheelis writes, ". . . if we invoke the leopard that can't change his spots, saying 'That's just the way I am, might as well accept it,' we abandon the freedom to change and exploit what we have been in the past to avoid responsibility for what we shall be in the future."[20]

Although there may be good reasons for a poor self-image, it doesn't follow that we must continue to perpetuate day by day the negative input of our inner critics. As difficult as it may be to change our old patterns of thinking, it *is* possible. You don't have to be bound by your past. Understanding this led a patient of Swiss psychiatrist Paul Tournier to write, "It is much easier to be in the position of a victim than in that of a person conscious of his responsibilities and of the gifts he is endowed with. But it is the only way to inner maturity."[21] And an improved self-image and heightened expectations for ourselves are essential steps toward effective management of our lives.

What will you place in the blanks after the words "I am"?

3

Why You Need
a Life
Purpose

The 25-Hour Woman misses the boat if she starts with
schedules and lists of things to do. Those particulars
are important, and knowing how to arrange them is
crucial to effective living. But the *sine qua non* of personal management is an even more basic element, too frequently overlooked: your very own sense of *purpose*.

Your purpose is your Grand Design—an "intended or desired result," according to one dictionary. It is what your life is
all about. It is your reason for living.

When I speak on time management and introduce this subject of purpose, hands shoot up and heads turn to neighbors for
clarification. "Do you mean 'goal' "?

No, I don't mean goal. Goals come next in the process of
management. But to avert confusion at the outset, I'll briefly
contrast goals and purpose.

Goals relate to *activity;* purpose relates to *aim.* One is the
what of your life; the other is the *why.* Goals are what you want
to *do;* purpose is what you will *be. While goals have to do with
specific achievements, purpose is concerned with the motivation
behind those achievements.* For example, if you said, "I want to

43

make a million dollars," you would have a goal. A purpose statement, on the other hand, might be: "I want to have a spirit of philanthropic giving." You can always be generous with what you have whether you are wealthy or poor. A goal, then, is limited by external factors, but a purpose is not. This is the most important distinction between a goal and a purpose: A goal depends on your circumstances; a purpose doesn't. You can't always control your life-style; but you *can* choose how you will live.

The Apostle Paul put purpose and goals in their proper perspective when he said, "So I run straight to the goal with purpose in every step. . . ."[1] A life purpose encompasses *all* your goals. So strive for goals, but set your mind on purpose.

If the idea of having purpose is new to you, you aren't alone. I meet a lot of people who have never thought in terms of an all-encompassing purpose for their lives. Some don't even want to!

One day when I signed in at the exercise club for my regular workout, the fellow behind the desk asked where I got the monogrammed sweatshirt I was wearing. I explained that a group of people I spoke to gave it to me as a gift of appreciation. His co-worker, decked out in colorful exercise garb, and checking herself in the mirror every five seconds, asked what I spoke on. I briefly responded, "I talked to them about how to have a purpose in life."

She eyed me strangely for a moment, then dismissed it with a shrug and a disinterested "oh" and adjusted her leotard.

Don't be concerned if your concept of life purpose is fuzzy. It will come into focus in time. As we explore it in more detail, we'll begin with four reasons why you should have an all-encompassing purpose to live by.

1. A purpose makes sense out of life.

The *Esquire* cover arrested my attention as I scanned a display of periodicals. It featured a striking young woman, with piercing, yet pathetically empty eyes. The caption beside her photo read: "I have a good job and a condo on the beach. I run four miles a day and play tennis twice a week. I'm in perfect health, and my roller skates cost $100. I guess you could say I'm . . . unhappy."[2]

Why is it that a person who seems to have everything has nothing to live for, while another person with less favorable odds can't get enough of life? The difference lies in whether or not they see meaning in their existence. Purpose gives that meaning that no possession or place in life can intrinsically offer. Even splendor turns stagnant if it is an end in itself. A purpose is vital to your well-being because it concerns you with the means of getting to the end. It reminds you that life is a process, and that the way you get where you're going is as important, and maybe more so, than where you go.

This *process mentality* toward life gives you meaning and motivation when the particulars of the moment raise doubts. Who of us has not at least once in our life wondered at the futility of our activities and achievements? Such times of questioning our endeavors, or even our very existence, are healthy because they force us to consider our purpose.

A friend once said to me, "You know, life is very daily." She wasn't complaining, but was simply coming to grips with the mundane maintenance that ate up most of her time. Acknowledging that cooking, cleaning, and carpooling left room for little else, she said, "I'd probably hang it all up if I couldn't see the bigger picture." Curious, I asked, "What's the bigger picture?" "Well," she reflected, "I've made a commitment to myself to live creatively at all levels, whether I'm tying shoelaces or trading stock." What she was saying was that she gave substance to her situations, rather than expecting her situations to give meaning to her. She has a process mentality toward life. It could be said of her what I read in an ad for a women's clothing line: "She's not just going places, she's there!"

Have you ever thought about how much of your life is given to repetitive tasks? Just this morning as I was going through the motions of making my bed, I said to myself, "I just did this!" Straightening, grooming, repairing, eating, sleeping—all sustain the status quo, yet show little in terms of accomplishment. And it isn't just menial chores that bewilder our being. Any work can become mundane if you do it with regularity but without real reason—even the highest-paying executive position.

It was wise and wealthy King Solomon who, according to most historians, penned the words "Vanity of vanities, all is vanity." Dr. Walter C. Kaiser, Jr., a professor of Semitic languages, says that Solomon was speaking to the burning issue in the hearts of people from the beginning of time: "the search for the worth, meaning, and goal of life."[3] In an analysis of the context of Solomon's declaration, Dr. Kaiser writes, "We must be careful not to mistake [his] use of 'vanity' for our own concepts of negativism, futility, and pessimism." The word *vanity* is more correctly translated "empty," and the " 'all' in the 'all is vanity' refers to all the activities of life rather than being a blanket declaration of the total uselessness of the universe." The main point Solomon is making, he concludes, is: "The purpose of life cannot be found in any one of the good things found in the world;" rather, while we should enjoy the gifts of life, we must find a "fixed point of reference for [our] own meaning."[4]

A purpose gives you that fixed point of reference in the dailiness (and dubiousness) of life. Not that it waves a magic wand over life's banes and banalities. But it does help you keep your head straight when everything looks cockeyed or counterproductive.

Remember: *Important activities don't make your life meaningful; a meaningful life makes your activities important.*

2. A purpose keeps you going.

Gail Sheehy wrote a sequel to her best-seller *Passages,* calling it *Pathfinders.* A "pathfinder" is a person who has "already met a test," someone who successfully navigated through a passage—a crisis period—and emerged better and stronger. She surveyed sixty thousand people between eighteen and eighty, and personally interviewed several hundred individuals.

There was one particularly clear-cut conclusion in her data: "The one constant in the lives of people who enjoy high well-being ... was a devotion to some cause or purpose beyond themselves."[5] Interestingly, she added this: "Given the contemporary cultural tilt, 'purpose' is the one element you or I might not have predicted as crucial to life satisfaction. Yet the results were dramatic. ... The distinction is so considerable that it makes the current pop philosophy of looking out for Number One sound like a national suicide pact."[6]

Crises come in all shapes and sizes. They can touch any area of your life—physical, financial, emotional, to name a few; and they can stop you dead in your tracks. When your plans go awry, you are apt to go to pieces if you can't see beyond what you have lost or incurred. As important as goals are, they aren't sure things. Nor is your skillfully arranged schedule. One change in circumstances can eliminate all of them and dramatically alter your life overnight. Though you should plan trips and projects and career ambitions, you have no guarantee that you will possess the physical, mental, and material resources to achieve them. What happens if a loved one dies, or an accident permanently disables you, or a financial disaster reduces your assets to the shirt on your back?

Viktor Frankl survived the Nazi concentration camps and wrote a remarkable account of his experience in *Man's Search for Meaning*. As he described the atrocities the prisoners suffered, he simultaneously dealt with the deeper attitudes they held. He became curious that, of those who were spared the crematorium or gas chamber, some survived, while others gave up and died or took their own lives. The former, he concluded, still held hope for the future; the latter had no reason to go on. He wrote, "Woe to him who saw no more sense in his life, no aim, no purpose, and therefore no point in carrying on. He was soon lost."[7]

A woman who had been widowed for eighteen months told me, "My main function for thirty-seven years was taking care of my husband and children. When he died, I lost my major function." She's just now beginning to define herself.

Purpose gives you a major function that is constant and certain. If you have to give up everyone and everything important to you, you can still hold to your reason for living. As Nietzsche said, "[S]he who has a why to live can bear with almost any how."

3. A purpose helps you feel significant.

A young mother once shared a moving experience with me. Shortly after her second child was born, the infant contracted a disorder that induced chronic diarrhea, requiring constant care. It persisted for a year and disrupted the whole household, particularly the mother's well-laid plans for those months. She had committed herself to substantial involvement in a local women's movement, and had to renege on her responsibilities.

At first she resented the unwelcomed intrusion. Then she sat back and studied the situation. What stood out in her mind was her fundamental desire to help women reach their full potential. Now it seemed that this thrust was thwarted because her commitment to carrying it out had to be canceled.

As she contemplated her disappointment, she looked at her older child, a three-year-old girl, and suddenly the light went on. She had an opportunity now that she would never again have once her child started school. Her daughter would be her protégée, her disciple. She talked with earnest enthusiasm of the very special time she had "mentoring" her little girl over that year, time she would not have given her had she been free to leave home and pursue other activities.

This woman is an illustration of what we talked about in chapter 2 regarding our need for self-worth. Your attitude, not your achievements, fosters your self-esteem, and a sense of purpose makes a vital contribution to your attitude. It's not the title you have, or where you work, or what you do, but your perspective that makes the difference.

The late William H. Mikesell, minister and psychologist, writing The Power of High Purpose, observed: "Purpose is the greatest asset of the human mind. It is the thing that tunes us up for a good performance. . . . Purpose is to the mind what

good health is to the body."[8] Your self-esteem and your purpose have an interdependent relationship. Like the chicken
and the egg, it's hard to tell which comes first. It may be that
affirming your worth will instinctively inspire a sense of purpose. On the other hand, you just may see yourself more
clearly once you have established your reason for being.

A sound purpose benefits you *and* others. Gail Sheehy said a
purpose answers the question "What's in it for me?" Then she
added: "That is only part of the story. What makes purpose
both so individually satisfying and so culturally necessary is
what is in it for society."[9] You make sense of your life when
you see what's in it for you. You feel significant when you see
your contribution to others. We're not talking about an ego
trip; we're talking about that essential drive to feel and feed
our "belongingness."

"A tragic aspect of the minor-purpose individual," wrote
Mikesell, "is that he does not feel close to mankind. People are
not close to him because he is not close to himself. Whether he
wants to be or not to be, he is a little island unto himself. He
also feels quite apart from God."[10] You can expect the reverse
to be equally true. When you solidify your purpose, you secure
your place in the sun—even if it is recognized only by yourself.

4. A purpose brings satisfaction.

We women often say, "It doesn't take much to satisfy me."
In one sense that is usually true. Most of us are pretty easy to
please. An occasional rose (it doesn't have to be a whole
dozen), a listening ear, a lingering cup of coffee, an encourag-
ing note from a friend—these happily fill that vague vacuum
we all experience from time to time. But I've seen something
else to be just as true: While it may not take much to satisfy us,
it doesn't last long either! As the saying goes, "I don't want
much, I just want more."

As quickly as we are pleased, we are discontented. Aristotle
observed, "It is the nature of desire not to be satisfied." We are
creatures of want. Of course, part of this proclivity is necessary
to our very survival. One meal doesn't last for life, and we'd all

starve to death if it weren't for a mechanism in our brain that periodically tells us we're hungry.

We also owe it to dissatisfaction that we aren't still living in the Stone Age. A nation totally content with the status quo would breed complacency and block progress. Individually, we would never develop to our full capacity apart from realizing there's more. I well recall when I got my first two-wheeler and my dad took on the task of weaning me from my tricycle. I wasn't satisfied anymore with the trike, but mastering the two-wheeler was scary. It must have been an ordeal because I remember praying, "God, if You'll just help me ride this bike, I'll never ask You for anything again." Of course I learned to ride the bike, and of course I didn't stop praying for help when I got dissatisfied with something else and wanted to change that. I suppose one way to look at life is to see it as changing dissatisfaction to satisfaction. The trouble with this approach, though, is that you don't gain ground, you lose it, living out the words of the song "Is that all there is?" The woman in that song gets what she wants, then doesn't want what she gets. She feels incomplete because something is missing in her life or herself. The crux of her chronic discontent is that who she is or what she has is *not enough*. So she continually sets herself up for disappointment.

I watched a television interview with the great actress Helen Hayes. Now in her eighties, she reflected on her career, and particularly the odds she overcame on the road to stardom. Her short stature and rather plain appearance worked against her, but her passion for the theatre and her confidence in her ability triumphed. When the interviewer brought up names of some of her glamorous contemporaries, Helen appeared sincerely sad and said that she has always felt sorry for the beauty queens. She went on to relate that, upon aging, some she knew became recluses. One had even refused to see Helen when the latter was near her home in Europe. Helen concluded that when they lost their youth and beauty, they lost their identity, thus their incentive.

Think about what fulfills you. Will it last? Or will time and events someday leave you empty-handed?

I cross-stitched a motto that reads: "I don't need a great deal of love—just a steady supply." Your purpose won't fill all your voids or fix your flaws. But, over the long haul, it *will* give you a steady supply of satisfaction.

Choosing Your Own Way

I heard someone say, "Everyone has a purpose for living; the tragedy of tragedies is that we would live and die, having never known our purpose."

You are living for something. If you don't establish what it is now, you may have regrets later. A wealthy businessman confessed, "I spent my whole life climbing the ladder of success only to get to the top and find out it was leaning against the wrong wall."

That doesn't have to happen to you. No one can arrogantly proclaim with the poet, "I am the master of my fate, I am the captain of my soul." But to a large degree, you *are* the designer of your destiny. Some women have a hard time with this concept because of a background or bias that runs contrary to thinking autonomously. For example, a Christian woman may see her role as one of living through a man—bowing to his decisions, dreams, and desires. To her, an independent thought smacks of selfishness and even sin. The Christian values that guide her role as wife and mother may seem to conflict with the role of an individual establishing her own life goals and priorities.

One such woman came to one of my seminars. We talked during a break, and she expressed her conflict. Something in her wanted very much to believe what I was saying; but something else said it was wrong. She had always understood that her life was to be an extension of her husband's, that his "calling" became her calling. Wouldn't it contradict her beliefs and conflict with her marriage if she did her own thing?

I felt deeply for her. Her struggle was quite visible, and her confusion not uncommon—even in this day and age. She wanted a sense of personal identity, but she confused thinking for herself with disregarding others, particularly her husband. Gradually she began to see that she would help, not hinder, her marriage by being her own person. She learned that formulating a purpose for her life and living true to her beliefs were not mutually exclusive. Her husband, she realized, had tried to tell her that, but it hadn't made sense until this moment. She even said, "I see now that I was causing him pressure by expecting him to live for both of us."

Another woman wrote of her new enthusiasm about life after a seminar because, for the first time, she had a sense of purpose. Before that, she said, "Purpose was something other people had."

Everyone can and should have a purpose for living. It won't pervade every waking moment or appease all your wants and woes. In fact, there will be times you'd like to ignore it altogether and forget about living for anything but the moment (which is all right, as long as the outcome is beneficial, and not destructive). But, once established, your purpose is there to draw on when you need it.

Viktor Frankl wrote that in the concentration camps he was stripped of all his possessions, including the very hair on his body. He said he learned that "everything can be taken from a man but one thing: the last of the human freedoms—to choose one's attitude in any given set of circumstances, to choose one's own way."[11]

When you determine that purpose, you choose your own way. You decide how you will live, and what will be more important to you than anything else. *Your purpose is what you give to life regardless of what life gives to you.*

There is no formula for finding this purpose, but there is a process that helps to bring it into focus. We'll look at that in the next chapter.

4

How to Arrive at a Life Purpose

Picture your eightieth birthday party: a delectable cake packed with colorful candles; a host of friends celebrating your life; a myriad of memories accumulated over the years.

Suddenly a stranger appears at your gathering and identifies himself as a representative from a New York publishing house. He says that his company wants to print your autobiography, and they have asked him to obtain some information from you today. Specifically, they want to know the title of your life story and at least five other headings.

The festivities quiet down, and everyone watches you, waiting to hear your response. What will you send back to the publisher?

Naming your autobiography is a start toward nailing down your purpose. The title you ascribe to your life has something to say about what you count most important and, therefore, what you are living for.

This purpose is your motif—like the background threads that weave a tapestry, or the recurring refrain that distinguishes a symphony. When Anne Morrow Lindbergh wrote of

53

cultivating a technique of living she added, "I want first of all—in fact, as an end to these other desires—to be at peace with myself. I want a singleness of eye, a purity of intention, a central core to my life that will enable me to carry out these obligations and activities as well as I can."[1] Purpose is that central core. Anne Morrow Lindbergh's autobiography could easily have been titled *At Peace With Myself*.

One of my college literature professors was fond of the works of Robert Browning, so we memorized many of his lines. One assignment I never forgot was from the poem "Rabbi Ben Ezra." It may be familiar to you:

> Grow old along with me!
> The best is yet to be,
> The last of life, for which the first was made:
> Our times are in His hand
> Who saith, "A whole I planned,
> Youth shows but half; trust God: see
>   all, nor be afraid!"

As well as I remember those words, I recall the professor's interpretation. He said, "In youth man stores up experience; in old age he begins to see God's design."

Most of you reading this are probably somewhere between youth and old age and have begun to see your design emerge—a design that evolves over time. Right now, let's explore the perspective that is vital to a lasting life purpose.

1. See the value of the past.

The morning sessions of the seminar I was attending had ended, and I joined a number of other conferees who waited in line to be seated for lunch. As we inched toward the dining room, I struck up a conversation with the couple behind me. Our chatting revealed that the husband was a pediatric dentist. I had never met a dentist who specialized in children and was curious about his profession. "Why," I asked, "did you choose this particular career?"

As though I said the magic word, or pressed the right button, he lit up and launched into an enthusiastic explanation. I learned that his parents died when he was seven, and he was subsequently taken into an orphanage. His memories of growing up there always sparked warm and thankful feelings because his guardians showed such love and care toward him. When he became a self-sufficient adult, he determined to repay the kindness demonstrated to him by helping other children whenever possible. He selected child dentistry because he could facilitate the development of good habits in their formative years. Even if he did not remain in dentistry, he said, he would find a way to influence young people.

He elaborated further, but I was still contemplating his earlier comments. Here was a man who had every reason to resent his lot in life. Not only did he lose his parents at a crucial age, but he was apparently overlooked for adoption and missed having a normal childhood. Yet it didn't occur to him to be bitter and feel sorry for himself. He was grateful and had discovered a compelling life aim largely out of appreciating his undesirable background rather than feeling sorry for himself.

The late Corrie ten Boom, the remarkable Dutch woman who suffered in concentration camps because she helped Jews to escape the Nazis, said, "Today I know that . . . memories are the key not to the past, but to the future. I know that the experiences of our lives, when we let God use them, become the mysterious and perfect preparation for the work He will give us to do."[2]

The experiences of your life—good *and* bad—set the stage for your own unique script. Together they shape your desires and direction. Adversity and prosperity are like colors on a canvas. Individually, one hue may please your eye more than another. But in combination, each shade contributes to the finished work of art.

History is replete with accounts of men and women whose hurts and handicaps inspired great dreams and accomplishments. Booker T. Washington, an overcomer in his own right, said, "Success is to be measured not so much by the position that one has reached in life as by the obstacles which he has overcome while trying to succeed."

One thing I've learned in life is this: Nobody has an ideal

past. But nobody has an unsalvageable one either. The biggest barrier to anyone's success is not mistakes or misfortune. It is succumbing to them. Don't forget that Babe Ruth himself struck out 1,330 times!

It's true, you may have irreversible limitations because of an accident or trauma. But you can even make that work for you if you are willing to see the redemptive qualities.

In the movie *The Natural,* Robert Redford portrayed Roy Hobbs, a gifted baseball player who signed with a major league team and headed for stardom. But through a bizarre twist of fate, his promising career crashed in an instant, and he went into oblivion for sixteen years. When he slowly came back into the public eye, he was reunited with his boyhood sweetheart. After hearing all that had happened to him, she reflected, "I believe we have two lives: the life we learn with and the life we live with afterward."

Whatever your past, you can learn something from it. You can't change it, but you can channel it for your good. I've met people who think it is too late to redeem the past, thus too late to realize a life purpose. They believe in the philosophy that "Life is like a Kleenex—it's not much good once you've blown it." Nothing is further from the truth. It is never too late.

Edith Schaeffer, wife of the late philosopher Francis Schaeffer, and cofounder with him of L'Abri—a spiritual retreat in Switzerland—recounted this lesson learned from a botched baking endeavor. A young girl named Jane was helping her prepare a meal for weekend guests, and she started on Edith's special sponge-cake recipe. Concerned by the looks of the batter, she took it to Edith, who immediately knew something was wrong. It was a strange mixture—yellow, sticky, and gluey. They reread the recipe and realized that she had overlooked the sugar, and it was too late to add it. Jane wanted to throw it out and start over. But Edith said no, they couldn't afford to, and she contemplated an alternative. What could they do with eggs, salt, baking powder, flour, and water?

That night the guests had, not sponge cake for dessert, but chicken noodle soup for dinner. And all thirty people exclaimed that they had never tasted better. Edith smiled across the table at Jane and remarked, "Not sponge cake, but marvelous noodles which are just as important. Don't ever forget this, Jane.

"Don't ever forget that if you can't be a 'sponge cake' because of having spoiled something which you can't go back and do over, the Lord can make you into marvelous 'noodles.' Just say it to yourself, anytime you feel you have 'blown it'—'I can't be a sponge cake now, but I can be noodles.' "[3]

2. Seek the challenge of the future.

Sören Kierkegaard said, "Life can only be understood backwards; but it must be lived forwards."

Television performer Norma Zimmer told of her disadvantaged childhood in her autobiography. Hardship and heartache touched most of her growing up years, and stressed the family relationships. After her parents died and her own children had grown up, she learned that her grandfather's farm, where she was raised, was turned into one of the largest silver mines in Idaho. Ironically, years before, her father had speculated that there might be silver there. She couldn't help but ponder "what might have been" if her father had struck it rich. Would her parents have loved each other more without the constant tension of poverty? Perhaps her father would not have become an alcoholic; her sister might have lived longer had she not been so malnourished. Then Norma concluded, "But we must live instead with what has been and even more important, with what is and may yet be."[4]

A might-have-been mentality obstructs the future. When you are obsessed with what-might-have-beens, you aren't free to pursue what-may-bes.

In a speech to the House of Commons, Winston Churchill said, "If we open a quarrel between the past and the present, we shall find that we have lost the future." The Apostle Paul wrote: ". . . one thing I do: forgetting what lies behind and reaching forward to what lies ahead, I press on. . . ."[5] You can't reach forward if you are bound backward. The word *forget,* in

the original Greek language that Paul used, means "to neglect." How do you neglect something? By ceasing to nurture
it. Paul didn't knock having memories; he rejected holding on
to them at the expense of growth and progress. In essence, his
advice concerning the past is, don't feed it!

Charley Boswell, former University of Alabama football
star, with hopes of a career in professional baseball, lost his
eyesight in World War II, and later became the National Blind
Golf Champion. He was quoted as saying, "I never count what
I've lost; I only count what I have left." Seeking the challenge
of the future is counting what you have left and moving on
from there.

3. Seize the opportunity in today.

The past has value, and the future holds promise. Yet both
must have their proper place. For today is where you are; and
while you can anticipate what may be, you can only appropriate what is.

I was teaching a seminar at a rustic mountain campground
and took advantage of an afternoon interlude to explore the
nearby town with a friend. We discovered an outdoor bazaar
and a merchant who was selling an impressive green house-
plant. Impressive, because it was full and sturdy; because it was
quite inexpensive; and because he said it would grow anywhere.

I had begun to feel like the all-time black thumb because my
plants were dying off one by one. So I couldn't resist this bargain. Proud of my purchase, I promptly placed it at a focal
point in my living room. Though it was guaranteed to be
nearly indestructible, I tended it with loving care. For several
weeks, I eyed it happily in my comings and goings. It added
such a nice touch to my decor.

Then one day my plant didn't look quite right. Its lovely
leaves seemed lifeless, and all my attempts to revive it failed. I
finally admitted it was beyond help and pitched it. Whatever
the reason, one thing was certain: That plant didn't prosper
where it was placed.

People are like plants. They either thrive where they are, or they don't. A common cliché tells an important truth: "Bloom where you are planted." Oswald Chambers put it another way: "Never allow the thought, 'I am of no use where I am;' because you certainly can be of no use where you are not." George Bernard Shaw wrote, "People are always blaming their circumstances for what they are. I don't believe in circumstances. The people who get on in this world are the people who get up and look for the circumstances they want, and, if they can't find them, make them." Either you will bide time waiting for the right circumstances, or you will make your circumstances right.

In 1978, Marvella Bayh, forty-six-year-old wife of United States Senator Birch Bayh, appeared on a talk show to share openly her struggle with cancer. Though she was in remission, she knew her days were numbered. The interviewer's last question was, "What is one thing you want to tell everyone who is watching this?" She replied, "If there's something important for anyone to do, they should do it now." Less than one year later she was dead.

An ancient saying warns:

> Four things come not back:
> The spoken word;
> The sped arrow;
> Time past;
> The neglected opportunity.

Don't let your opportunities slip through your fingers.

4. Sense the uniqueness that sets you apart.

In the book *Celebrate Your Self,* Dorothy Briggs lays out mind-boggling mathematical calculations that put to rest any notion of finding another person like yourself in this universe. She concludes, "The likelihood of another genetically put together into your unique pattern at any time in the past, anywhere today or any time in the future is so infinitesimally small as to be inconceivable. And this uniqueness is quite apart from all the conditioning that has been reacted to by this uniqueness of yours. To say that you are a special event in the universe is not Pollyanna drivel. It is a fact of life."[6]

Commenting on individuality, Congresswoman Barbara Jordan observed, "People always want you to be born where you are. They want you to have leaped from the womb a public figure. It just doesn't go that way. I am the composite of my experience and all the people who had something to do with it."[7]

Why is your uniqueness important to your choice of purpose? Because only you know the components of your composite, and only you can catch that common thread that has been weaving the fabric of your life.

I am always moved, but not surprised, by women's responses as they write out their life purpose during a seminar. When they choose to share it with the group, they often do so with great intensity. Why the strong emotional overtone? Because embodied in a simple statement is a complexity of convictions and experiences that touches the deepest level of one's being. What sounds merely nice or noble to one person may hold miles of meaning for another.

When I think of a life purpose, I picture the best and the worst situations. For example, imagine yourself luxuriating in an exquisite estate, surrounded by a loving family and a host of servants. Then think of living in a refugee camp, subject to squalor and starvation. If you can realize your purpose in both places, you have something worth living for.

Many a statement of purpose can satisfy those conditions; but it must satisfy *you*. You can't pull a purpose out of a hat. Moreover, you can't force or fake it. You must find it deep within you, and that may require some hard soul searching. But if you want it enough, you'll get it. If you don't know your life purpose but want to, ask God to help you find it. The psalmist said, "Thou [God] wilt make known to me the path of life . . ." (Psalms 16:11 NAS).

Your purpose may be stated in one sentence, or it may fill a paragraph. It may come together in a number of ways. Some tell me they have determined their purpose by observing a mentor or other exemplary person. Others adopt striking words from inspirational reading; for example, many women say they have latched on to a particular verse in the Bible. Still others derive their purpose from their own assemblage of thoughts. Rose Kennedy, matriarch of the famous Kennedy clan, made a lifelong vow as a school girl "to hold my soul free in the face of changes of fortune." She has lived out that aim with dignity into her nineties, having experienced both the sweet and sour sides of life. A psychiatric nurse in one of my seminars gave her purpose as: "Learning to love and express love in all aspects of my life."

Your purpose may not seem unusual to others, but it will be unique to you. It has nothing to do with grandiose goals, lofty achievements, or universal fame. It is the quiet confidence that, even if you never leave your neighborhood, you will have lived fully.

5. Settle on a single-minded aim.

When Dr. Henry Kissinger was secretary of state, he was asked how he handled moments of crisis. He responded that "people who are obsessed with the uncertainty of events become exhausted emotionally. Everyone aspiring to high office probably needs a touch of monomania; in uncertain situations, without that self-confidence, you will destroy yourself."[8]

His insight has value for each of us, because we are all subject to crises and uncertainties. The dictionary defines *monomania* as "pathological obsession with one idea; intent concentration on, or exaggerated enthusiasm for a subject or an idea." Suggested synonyms are "fixation, compulsion, drive, fixed idea, one-track mind."

When the Apostle Paul said, "This one thing I do . . ." he certainly didn't mean he engaged in one activity and no more. We know from the accounts of his travels that he was occupied with many commitments. But he was *pre*occupied with one cause that subordinated everything else. A different translation of the same verse reads, "I am bringing all my energies to bear on this one thing." What Paul might have said, if I may put words in his mouth, was, "I do many things, but I desire one end."

Crystallizing Your Purpose

In my seminars participants think through their life purpose with the help of a worksheet like the one shown on page 63. You can do the same by dividing an 8½" x 11" piece of paper into three sections, and labeling them "Past," "Future," and "Present." Write whatever comes to your mind, even if it doesn't seem to connect with anything. You will be surprised at how a pattern will emerge as you let your thoughts flow. The questions on the worksheet are there to spark your thinking if you need help getting started.

Centering Your Life

Rabbi Liebman wrote, "We should remember the difference between the two meanings of 'end' which are found in the human language: the one 'finis' and the other 'telos.' Death has often written 'finis' to a life that has had no 'end,' no 'purpose.' The worst tragedy that can befall a human being is to come to the end (finis) without ever having possessed any end (telos)—without ever having sought for any great aim in the midst of his life career."[9]

I watched an artisan mold a lump of clay. As he worked, he said that the key to making successful pottery is "centering." Once you center the clay on the wheel, he explained, you can determine where you will go with it.

The 25-Hour Woman has many commitments, pulling her this way and that. But we can liken her life to that lump of clay. Once she centers on a purpose, once she possesses a telos, she has a technique with which to live out her destiny.

Life Purpose Worksheet

Past

In the past certain people and experiences influenced your thinking and helped mold your character. Write down the significant ones that come to mind.

When do you remember first feeling a sense of destiny?

What kind of life did you envision for yourself?

Have any of your dreams been fulfilled? How has this affected you?

Future

How do you see yourself in 1 year? 10 years? 30 years?

If you could do or be anything, what would it be? Why?

What will happen to your perspective if your circumstances change (e.g., if you become widowed or divorced)?

What will happen to your perspective if your circumstances *don't* change? (e.g., if you want to marry, but don't)?

Present

What are you doing now to bring about the dreams you have had in the past?

Have any of your desires changed? How? Why?

What are your convictions about how you will live? (i.e., have you made decisions you can't compromise?)

How do you feel about your present circumstances? Do you see them as a help or hindrance to your success?

PART TWO

What Do You Want out of Life?

In the long run (people) hit only what they aim at.

THOREAU

5

Why Goals
Are Important

"The word *goal* freezes me." The woman's voice was as cold as her choice of words, and she didn't know I heard her. She was attending a time-management seminar and, as we broke for coffee, I announced that the next session would be on goal setting.

Actually, I had my eye on this lady from the start, because she glared at me the bulk of the time. Her scowls communicated loudly and clearly that she had some beefs with time management. I knew where she was coming from, and was glad she was at the conference, even if someone had dragged her there. I was confident she would leave smiling, and she did.

Does the word *goal* freeze you? Or does it even sound familiar? Perhaps you have never given it a thought. Or perhaps, like many I meet, that's *all* you've done.

Years ago a couple I knew were cajoling their precocious three-year-old to eat his untouched dinner. When all attempts failed, they resorted to the old standby: "Think of all the starving children in China." Unmoved, the child flashed back, "Name one!"

How many times have you heard, "You need a goal"? If you're the compliant type, you probably have made a list, resurrected it every New Year's Day, and felt guilty in between.

If you are more the rebellious sort, you more than likely resisted the imperative just on principle.

Has anyone ever explained *why* you need a goal? You will never wholeheartedly commit yourself to one until you first understand what it can do for you. Goals are meant to benefit you, not to give you a hard time. Here are five good reasons to have a goal.

1. Goals reinforce your life purpose.

Proverbs advises us, "Dreaming instead of doing is foolishness." Someone quipped that there are three kinds of people: those who make things happen, those who watch things happen, and those who say, "What happened?" Goals put meat on the bones of your purpose and make things happen.

Suppose your purpose centers on philanthropy, an example I mentioned earlier. You feel a leaning toward an altruistic aim and wish to express it as a benevolent benefactor. Do you diligently plan a financial strategy, or do you hope for a windfall? Do you give to charity from the little you have, or do you wait until you have more? In other words, what are you specifically doing *now* to realize your purpose?

If you aren't doing anything, you may be afflicted with Someday Sickness. I had a friend who suffered incurably from this dread disease. We often shared our hopes and dreams and encouraged each other toward accomplishing them. She talked excitedly about making her life count, and doing great things *someday*.

Eventually we both moved to different parts of the country, but had opportunities to get together occasionally over the next few years. Each time, she discounted her present activities as temporary, and talked instead of what she planned to do *someday*. Then we lost contact.

Several years passed and one evening I was surprised to receive a phone call from her. As we chatted, I asked what she was doing. She said she didn't want to bother talking about that, because she was soon going to do something else. I told her I was happy for her and wished her success. About ten minutes after I hung up, I realized that what she told me were the very things she was "going to do" eight years ago, ten years ago, twelve years ago. Someday!

A sign in my exercise spa says, "It has been scientifically proven that thinking about it has yet to get anyone in shape." Thinking about your purpose won't make it happen. A goal will take your purpose out of the someday and bring it to today.

I once read, "Dreaming about a thing in order to do it properly is right; but dreaming about it when we should be doing it is wrong." There's a time to dream, and a time to do. In fact, the key is dreaming *and* doing.

David McClelland, the Harvard psychologist who has done research on high achievers, has found that they all have one common trait: They fantasize incessantly about how to achieve what they want. But they don't stop there; they *act* on their dreams.

Without a purpose, your activities are ends in themselves. But without goals, your purpose is little more than a dream.

2. Goals help you to know where you are going.

During her adventures in Wonderland, Alice encountered the Cheshire Cat at a fork in the road.

"Cheshire-Puss, would you tell me, please, which way I ought to go from here?"

"That depends a good deal on where you want to get to," said the Cat.

"I don't much care where—" said Alice.

"Then it doesn't matter which way you go," said the Cat.

"—so long as I get somewhere," Alice added as an explanation.

"Oh, you're sure to do that," said the Cat, "if you only walk long enough."

If you live long enough, you'll get somewhere. The question is, where? A close counterpart to Someday Sickness is the Somewhere Syndrome. The Somewhere Syndrome is described in a poem from my favorite childhood book. Here is part of it:

> Would you tell me the way to Somewhere?
> Somewhere, Somewhere,
> I have heard of a place called Somewhere—
> But know not where it can be.
> It makes no difference
> Whether or not
> I go in dreams
> Or trudge on foot,
> Or this time tomorrow
> How far I've got,
> Summer or Winter,
> Cold, or hot,
> Where, or When
> Or Why, or What—
> Please, tell me the way to Somewhere—
> The Somewhere meant for me.[1]

If you leave your future to fate, you have the Somewhere Syndrome. Rather than specify what you want out of life, you hope to stumble across it. The problem with that is, if you don't know what you want, you won't recognize it when you see it.

Before I make this point in my seminars, I illustrate it with a little exercise. I ask everyone to draw a "glip." When they look confused, and turn to one another inquisitively, I remain straight-faced and insist that they cooperate. So they begin to make marks on their papers. After a few minutes I tell them to compare their drawing with the others at their table, and to determine who has sketched the best glip. By now they are all laughing and guessing at the moral of my madness.

At this writing, the word *glip* is not in the English language, so everyone is hard pressed to draw one (though conferees have come up with some pretty creative attempts). Had I asked them to draw a tree, or an apple, or a house, no one would have had a problem identifying reasonable facsimiles. Everyone knows what a tree, apple, and house look like.

The lesson should be obvious: If you don't have a clear picture of what you want to accomplish, you won't know when you've accomplished it. Baseball great Yogi Berra is credited with saying, "If you don't know where you're going, you'll probably end up somewhere else." That's it in a nutshell!

How would you like to embark on a trip with no direction or destination? Such a serendipitous adventure might prove exciting once or twice in a lifetime. But would you want to spend every vacation that way? Yet that is exactly what many people do with their lives.

You have probably seen the television commercial in which someone eats a fattening food, then regretfully exclaims, "Wow, I could have had a V-8!" You may have a similar reaction if you leave your life to chance and take the first thing that comes along. I'm all for spontaneity; setting goals does not imply cementing a strict life plan. Goals are simply *decisions* about where you are going. They answer the question "Would you tell me the way to Somewhere?"

3. Goals help you to make wise choices.

An entrepreneur launched a new enterprise and hired a leading artist to design an insignia for his firm. When he received the completed artwork, he was very pleased. It was just what he wanted—plain and to the point. As he admired it, the bill fell out. Shocked by the amount, he called the artist and asked, "Why is the price so high when the design is so simple?" The artist answered, "The price is for knowing what to leave out."

Goals are for knowing what to leave out. They are a filtering system for all the opportunities and demands that bombard you. When you say yes to a vital few alternatives, you say no to the many others. Goals aren't meant to *complicate* your life; rather, they should *concentrate* it. People are apt to think of goals as *adding* to an already too-full pile. Actually, wisely set goals will probably *subtract* from it.

I watched an interview with actor Paul Newman, who is known for his many other pursuits, such as car racing, politics, and the food business. He had just celebrated his fifty-ninth birthday. Sensing the value of life in a new way, he decided to slow down and narrow his interests. When the interviewer asked him what he thought was his greatest accomplishment thus far, Paul groped for a moment, then said that he could have achieved so much more by doing less.

Goals are friends, not foes. They protect you from doing more than you effectively can. I once heard an excellent piece of advice: "Say no once a day just to keep in practice." Goals help you say no to doing too many things, and they help you say no to doing the wrong things. Activity is wrong if it keeps you from doing what is more important. Back in the eighteenth century Voltaire warned, "The best is the enemy of the good." If you don't have a goal, you won't necessarily waste your life away or turn to criminal conduct. Good or bad is seldom the issue. The line more often falls somewhere between good, better, and best.

This principle has something to say not only about achievement goals, but also acquisition goals. I encourage women to keep a "wish list" of major items they hope to have—furniture, a special piece of clothing, a vacation, a home. Some people smart at the idea, thinking it would promote a materialistic perspective. Actually, it has the opposite effect.

Planning your purchases guards against greed and impulse buying. It is easier to pass up frivolous bargains and forego immediate pleasures when you know something better is down the line.

I was in a friend's home one evening, and the conversation turned to real estate. She took out a bulging photo album and showed me pictures and floor plans of two types of homes she had her eye on: one, a split-level, solar-heated house she wanted to buy if she stayed in Southern California; the other, a traditional colonial style, if she moved back to the South. I was impressed by the homework she had done, and then I noticed that her album also had pictures of campers, Jacuzzis, and speedboats (she's a waterskiing buff).

"What a clever idea," I commented. She grinned and reminded me that four years earlier at a time-management seminar, I advocated a wish list. She went one step better and turned it into a wish book. It had had a great impact on her financial state. Whereas she previously spent money beyond her means and accrued enormous finance charges, she has since destroyed her credit cards and is gradually getting out of debt. With these big goals in front of her, she said, she thinks twice before she buys anything now. "It's been fun," she offered. "Who knows what will happen?"

I can remember when the standard ice-cream choices were vanilla, chocolate, and strawberry. Now it's thirty-one flavors or more. Similarly, the options available to us in a lifetime are overwhelming.

How do you spell relief? G-O-A-L!

Before you move on to the next point, say no five times—just to start practicing.

4. Goals help you to see progress.

"I didn't do one thing today." Sound familiar? You've probably said it more than once. Truth is, as long as you are breathing and brushing your teeth, you are doing something. In fact, on the days you say that, you probably do more than usual. But your frustrating admission implies that you did nothing productive.

The difference between mere activity and meaningful accomplishment is progress. Progress means headway and achievement. None of us likes to spin our wheels and get nowhere. We want something to show for our efforts. We all need checkpoints in our lives when we can pat ourselves on the back because we've moved from one place to another. Goals can serve as those checkpoints. They assure us that we really are getting somewhere.

There's an old Chinese proverb that goes, "A journey of a thousand miles must begin with a single step." Many people never take that first step, so they never have the satisfaction of arriving anywhere. They either don't believe that a single step can make a difference; or, there are so many places they want to go, they can't decide where to head first. Either way, they end up going nowhere. Doing something is always better than doing nothing. You'll be surprised how the little steps add up to big strides, and how inches turn into miles.

I talked with a Hollywood scriptwriter who told me that he was reading the modern classics. As I inquired further, he said he read for ten minutes a day. I chuckled, thinking he was surely joking. But he was dead serious. "I read ten minutes a day because that's all I can handle at one sitting." (I thought of all the times I gave up on an erudite piece of work and opted for something lighter.) "Are you getting anywhere?" I asked skeptically. "Oh, yes. I just finished *War and Peace.*" It took a year, but he got through it. Now he is working on *The Rise and Fall of the Roman Empire.*

A goal need not be big and complex. It can be small and simple. What is important is that, however slowly, it takes you from where you are to where you want to be.

Maxwell Maltz gave one of his patients this good advice:

> Functionally, a man is somewhat like a bicycle. . . . A bicycle maintains its poise and equilibrium only so long as it is going forward towards something. You have a good bicycle. Your trouble is you are trying to maintain your balance sitting still, with no place to go. It's no wonder you feel shaky. We are engineered as goal-seeking mechanisms. We are built that way. When we have no personal goal which we are interested in and which "means something" to us, we are apt to "go around in circles". . . . Get yourself a goal worth working for. . . . Always have something ahead of you to "look forward to."[2]

Edward Griggs, a Stanford University professor at the turn of the century, and a popular lecturer on the subject of personal growth, determined that "fifteen minutes a day devoted to one definite study will make one a master in a dozen years." Who of us cannot give fifteen minutes a day to a worthwhile goal?

The greatest hindrance to achieving goals is not too little time;

it is too many excuses. Everyone has limitations and each stage of life has restrictions. There will always be reasons why you can't do what you want to do. But there will never be an ideal time. Progress, like everything else we've talked about, is a process. When will you start the process, if not now? When you find a better job? When you buy a bigger house? When you get married? When the babies are out of diapers? When the kids start school? When you retire?

A friend of mine who is a grandmother came to a seminar and said to me later, "Sybil, please tell those busy moms it isn't any easier when the kids are grown and gone. I got more accomplished when I had three preschoolers than I do now. Then, time was more precious, so I *had* to make it count. Now that I have more for myself, I'm not as careful with it and I end up not doing the things I really want to do."

Single or married, parent or childless, working in the home or outside, the process toward progress starts *now.* Set a goal, stick to it, and you will see that progress.

> Progress, man's distinctive mark alone,
> Not God's, and not the beasts': God is, they
>   are;
> Man partly is, and wholly hopes to be.
>   ROBERT BROWNING

5. Goals help you to tap your talent.

When John F. Kennedy was president, he was asked, "What do you think makes for happiness?" He answered, simply, that he believed the key to happiness was doing what you do best.

An ambitious woman came to a seminar already "burned out" on goal setting. She rolled out her list of goals like a scroll, told me she was at her wit's end, and asked for help. I looked at her list and, momentarily forgetting her frustration, laughed.

"What's funny?" she moaned.

"I'm sorry," I apologized. "I'm not laughing at you; I'm laughing with you, because I was in the same boat. What you have here is a rehabilitation program."

Over the years I have counseled other goal "victims," and many have something in common. I recognize it because I share their tendency. And I love to talk about it at seminars because I see instant relief all around the room.

Listen carefully, because this is one of the most valuable pieces of information you will get in this book: People who suffer goal burnout often focus on their weaknesses instead of their strengths. So they start on a negative note, and end on a worse one, because their goals are glaring reminders of how inadequate they are. They are doubly defeated because they have far more goals than anyone could ever tend to.

Have you ever been asked to list your positive and negative traits? Which list is longer? Most people are in touch with a lot of their flaws, but hard pressed to name but a few virtues. So if you establish goals to correct all your shortcomings, you have set an impossible task.

Certainly goals can serve to overcome a handicap—such as learning to walk again after a debilitating accident. But they were never meant to overhaul your life. They should enhance and enrich it.

I once thought I should pursue the field of counseling because my work put me in so many counseling situations. So I set a number of related goals, including a reading program, psychology courses, and counseling seminars. My endeavors were interesting but equally frustrating. The shoe just didn't fit.

It was a wonderful day when I acknowledged I was not skilled as a counselor and removed it from my list of lifetime goals. Relief was immediate—I no longer felt the pressure of continually falling short of my goal. I still value the field of counseling and explore it in occasional reading and in conversations with friends and colleagues who are gifted in that area. But it is not a major thrust in my life.

How do you know if you are tapping a talent or tormenting a weakness? By answering the question "Does this encourage me and lead to growth and development, or does it discourage me and get me nowhere?" Both require your best efforts and hard work. But one energizes while the other enervates. Your adrenaline should flow freely when you do what you do well. Noted psychologist B. F. Skinner was asked when he was seventy-nine, "Has aging ever depressed you?"

"No," he responded. "Depression comes from discouragement at not having anything to do that you do well. The solution is to find something to be successful at."[3]

What do you do well? More important, are you doing it?

It appears that women struggle with this more than men. Through traditional upbringing and conventional role models, they equate femininity with passivity and, in the words of Archie Bunker, stifle themselves. Advertising executive Lois Wyse has said that men are taught to apologize for their weaknesses, women for their strengths. Though this is changing, a woman is still less apt to be in touch with what she can do than a man, or less apt to use it for personal satisfaction.

In the Academy Award–winning movie *Chariots of Fire*, Olympic runner Eric Liddell told his sister, "God made me for a purpose and He made me fast, and when I run I feel His pleasure."

You may not be a gold-medal winner, but your Creator put some pretty special stuff in you, too, and He most likely smiles when you do something with it. He certainly can't be very pleased when you bury it. A commercial for hair products says, "If you don't look good, we don't look good." False humility—the I-am-nothing disposition—doesn't make God look very good. Who wants to believe in Someone who creates flops?

Everyone benefits when you employ your abilities. Veteran actress Bette Davis was asked about her earlier years in show business, and particularly about another actress who was reported to be her rival. Was she ever jealous of her costars? Quite emphatically she said no, that she wanted everyone to be their best because it make her look good!

A New York attorney and women's activist credited a special group of people with her success. She identified seventeen men and women in her "support system," including her car

mechanic, butcher, babysitter, secretary, grocer, and so forth—
all of whom she could count on, and who freed her time for responsibilities at home and work.

When you do "your thing," you help others do "their thing."
I saw a short ad in the classifieds that said, "Hauling is my
calling." Everyone does something well and worth being proud
of. The Apostle Peter said, "God has given each of you some
special abilities; be sure to use them to help each other . . ." (1
Peter 4:10 TLB). When you capitalize on your talents, you help
others capitalize on theirs. We all need that "support system."

Some persons never find their unique ability because they
are too busy fretting over their *in*abilities. If you are one of
those, you need to stop thinking about what you *can't* do, and
start exploring what you *can* do. I used the word *tap* with regard to your talent, because no one arrives overnight. You
have to begin somewhere. You can't strike oil unless you start
drilling. And you won't find your talent until you start tapping.

I read that when Walt Disney died, he left enough ideas on
the drawing board to keep his enterprise busy for a decade.
You may not be a genius on the level of Disney, but your gifts
are no less limited. Talent begets talent. You can't use it up;
you can only generate more.

If you haven't discovered your gold mine, start digging!

6

How to Set Achievable Goals

“I tried having a goal once,” a woman said to me, “but it didn’t work.” I had heard it before, and I believed it each time. Unless a goal meets certain criteria, it *won’t* work. But when it follows given guidelines, you will soon turn sentimental wishes into specific achievements and exchange fantasy for fulfillment.

A goal should satisfy seven tried-and-true requirements. When you set a goal, and it passes on each count, then you have a goal that is guaranteed to work.

1. A goal must be written.

The people at Success Motivation Institute say that if your goals are in writing, you are much more likely to accomplish them. A motivational speaker goes a step further and maintains, “If you don’t write it, you won’t do it.”

Writing something down doesn’t make it happen, but it does cause you to think about it more. Somehow the pen that puts a goal on paper makes an impression on your mind and keeps it on your “back burner.” If it isn’t on paper, it will probably fade away with the rest of your good intentions.

When you write down a goal, you are saying, “I am serious about this. I really want to achieve it.” Though no one else

79

may ever know about it, you are making a pact with yourself. When I first got into goal setting, I wrote down a five-year goal to "learn a winter sport." Next to it on my novice goal worksheet I put a short-range goal of "try skiing one more time." I had had one very bad experience and thought I should give it another chance before dropping it from the alternatives altogether. For the next couple of years other goal areas took priority and, frankly, I was still skittish about the slopes, so I didn't look for an opportunity to return to them.

Then I participated in a conference in Colorado with some of my colleagues. We were near a variety of ski areas, and scheduled one free day for the skiing enthusiasts among us. At once I was torn. Here was a perfect chance to accomplish my goal; but my tailbone smarted at the very thought of another impact with packed snow. So I halfheartedly talked myself out of it, saying, "This is a good chance to catch up on some work and take a nap." But my friends had other ideas. After breakfast they headed to the buses and said, "C'mon, Sybil, you'll love it." Wanting to, but not wanting to, I said rather unconvincingly, "I can't go; I don't have ski clothes."

A friend flew to her room, and came back with a parka and overalls. "I brought two sets," she said as she helped me change and whisked me to the bus.

My second attempt was so much fun I didn't want to leave. And I'm happy to report that my tailbone stayed intact. I doubt I would have gone if I hadn't been prompted by a written goal (and an unrelenting friend). In the end, I knew I owed it to myself to take advantage of a golden opportunity.

If you don't write down a goal, you have that much less incentive to achieve it and may lean toward Scarlett O'Hara's philosophy—"I'll think about that tomorrow."

2. A goal must be measurable.

When I taught grade school, I wrote a lot of lesson plans. Our principal was a stickler for teaching by objectives and periodically reviewed our plans without warning. He looked for written statements that specified the measurable intent for each class period. He subscribed to the principle that "an instructor will function in a fog of his own making until he knows just what he wants his students to be able to do at the end of the instruction."[1]

If your goal is too general, you will function in a fog, too. And you may miss the satisfaction of accomplishing it, because you will never be sure if you have. Let's say you have a goal "to read more." What is more? On the other hand, suppose your goal is to read one best-seller a month. Now you know exactly if and when you have accomplished it.

A friend of mine set out to needlepoint eight antique chair seats, as part of a broader goal to decorate her dining room. Her mother did two for her, so she had six to complete. Initially, she told me, she just worked on them when she found "extra" time. In two years, eleven months, she had done two and one-half canvases. She was discouraged, and "decided to make a commitment to getting it done."

She determined she would have to do one skein of yarn a week to finish by the following Christmas. She dated each skein, and gave herself two weeks off for the current holiday season. When I saw her in May, she was right on target, even though they were selling their home and packing boxes to move. "I take time to do it," she said. "We'll still get everything done and move." Then she added, "I haven't met all my other goals—I've fallen short. But I'm so much further ahead than I was."

When you are specific about your goals, you are more certain about the outcome. And you must be specific about the achievement itself, not the amount of time you put into it. Had my friend set a goal of needlepointing two hours a week, what promise would she have had of finishing her chairs? It's not how much time you spend at something that counts—unless, of course, you are in a competition that measures speed. It's what you get done that determines your success. So a goal should always be stated in terms of *results,* not efforts.

3. A goal must be challenging.

Challenge: "the quality of requiring the use of one's abilities, energy, or resources."

When did you last accomplish something that required your best shots? Maybe you haven't realized a goal because you haven't set your sights high enough. Robert Browning wrote, "Ah, but a man's reach should exceed his grasp, or what's a heaven for?"

A woman asked me, "Does every goal have to be lofty?" No, that is a trap that keeps you from achieving any goal at all. Challenging is not synonymous with grandiose. Goals don't need to set the world on fire. But they must spark your energies.

I know a twenty-two-year-old fellow who cleans the local franchise of a national restaurant chain. He works hard, and it shows. The place always sparkles. One day I told George how impressed I was by his conscientiousness. He beamed proudly, and said that for his efforts he had won a first place award in Southern California, and third in the state. I asked him where he saw himself going in the future; and he answered decisively. His goal is to supervise a janitorial service for a school system or a convalescent facility. But to do that, he wants more experience, including "another year here to get real good." He also takes classes at night to fulfill his high school requirements and wants to go on to college.

A lot of people would not be challenged by George's goal. But that is unimportant. What matters is that it challenges him. In the book titled *The Truth About You* the authors explain their process for helping people find their career niche. They review a person's autobiographical achievements, from early childhood to the present, and look for a recurring pattern, or design. The key, they say, is to identify accomplishments that the person felt were done well, and that resulted in a feeling of satisfaction, "regardless of their degree of significance in other people's eyes."[2]

You don't set goals to impress others; you set goals to inspire yourself. Nor do you set goals to imitate accomplishments of people you admire. Just because your friend is teaching her preschooler to play the violin by the Suzuki method, or returning to school, or entering the Pillsbury Bake-off is no reason for you to do the same, unless it is what you really want.

Goals should stem from intrinsic desires, call forth your best efforts, and instill a personal sense of pride. When they do that, they are challenging.

4. A goal must be believable.

If a goal set too low won't inspire your efforts, neither will a goal that is set too high. Both keep you neutralized in "no-man's land." James Thurber won our hearts with *The Secret Life of Walter Mitty*, a story about a weak-willed, henpecked man who fantasized incessantly. His wild imaginings never materialized into anything, because he concocted experiences way beyond his limitations. His dreams were little more than escapes.

Most of us have Walter Mitty moments. Mine come when I watch the Olympics and have illusions of sailing across the ice or scaling the bars with the grace and dexterity of the gold-medal skaters and gymnasts. But I don't entertain such ideas for long, because I know I could never follow through. A goal that is not in the realm of the conceivable is merely a castle in the sky. There's no solid ground there to plant your feet firmly on.

You can't lie to yourself. If you don't have an ear for foreign languages, it doesn't make sense to want to be an interpreter at the United Nations. You must believe you can accomplish what you dream of doing. Goals are dreams, not delusions.

A mother of three demanding children decided she wanted "to be able to teach piano" as a long-range personal goal. That was pretty challenging, considering she hadn't tickled the ivories for a number of years. But it was also believable. She would have shrunk at the goal of concert pianist, but she knew she had the ability to develop her skills sufficiently to instruct others.

She wrote down the following goals:

By next year: Learn ten pieces.
                      Perform in the National Music Teachers' Guild.

Immediate steps: Find a good teacher.
                   Play last piece played as a teenager.
                   Perform at an adult recital.

When I talked to her, she had accomplished her immediate goals, including the recital, where "I was successful, even though I didn't play well." She succeeded because she believed she could do it, and she did. She's on her way to that aim of teaching. And who knows? As she progresses closer to her goal, she just may start believing in bigger ones. She may end up on the concert circuit yet!

Somewhere between possible and impossible is the realm in which you should set your goals. When you combine the guidelines of "challenging" and "believable," you have what a minister of mine used to call "being intelligently in over your head."

An ancient philosopher said, "Do not think what is hard for you to master is humanly impossible; but if a thing is humanly possible, consider it to be within your reach." *Consider* is the key. Line up your possibilities and ask, "Can I see myself achieving this?" If you can, you have a believable goal.

5. A goal must be consistent.

One of my interests is natural foods preparation, including baking. With the help of marvelous equipment, I grind my own grain and produce homemade breads, rolls, pizza, and more. The health benefits are tremendous, plus it's just plain fun. In fact, I enjoy it so much that I became a dealer for the company that markets the machines. It seemed like a good opportunity to help people with nutrition and earn extra income at the same time. I designed a brochure to advertise my availability to do home demonstrations and invested in necessary materials. I even attended a two-day sales seminar.

Shortly after launching the endeavor, I told a publishing agent of my plans to expand my time-management seminars and to write this book. At one point in the conversation I happened to mention my new "extracurricular" activity. He looked at me in disbelief and said, "You're doing what?"

I repeated it and added that "I enjoy it, and do it well, and it's a good break from my mental work." He just shook his head and mumbled something like, "You should be writing that book every free minute you have."

He was right, but I didn't admit it for two months. When I took on bread-making demonstrations, I violated an important criterion of goal setting. My new pursuit, however worthwhile, caused a conflict of interests and interfered with more important goals I was already committed to. It was not consistent with my desire to start a business and publish a book.

I knew better, but I got off track. It's easy to do, even for an experienced time manager. I still bake for myself and friends; but I don't give up precious evenings and weekends to sell the idea to others. Perhaps someday I will, but now is not the time.

When you establish a goal, you must ask, "Is it compatible with my other goals and priorities?" If you are planning a trip to Europe and you have a tight budget, you may need to think twice before you buy new carpeting. Or, you may need to postpone the trip if your floor coverings are threadbare. If you aspire to a management position at your job, this may not be the best year to start a family, and vice versa.

Advocates of goal setting often appeal to the principle of "balance." A balanced life sounds like a good idea, but how realistic is it? Can a person really give equal time to every priority? I don't think so. But neither do I think that's what balance is all about.

At one point when I was killing myself to cover all the bases, I visited my dentist. As I lay in the chair and submitted to the drill, I looked at the ceiling and studied a mobile hanging there. Suddenly I saw something significant about its structure: None of the dangling figures were the same size or shape. Yet the mobile was perfectly balanced.

In the same way, the key to a balanced life is *compatible* parts, not *identical* parts. Here, consistency is a function not of equality but of harmony.

Harmony means "agreement" and "pleasing interaction." It suggests complementary relationships. Sometimes goal harmony is quite obvious, as in the example of a woman who came to a time-management seminar with no experience in goal setting. She was eager to learn, but unsure of herself. The idea of a goal seemed rather sophisticated to someone whose simple life-style seldom went beyond her small rural town.

When the conferees worked on their goal charts, she drew a blank. I reviewed some principles, reminded the women that goals need not be fancy, and encouraged them to build on what they were already doing. Suddenly this woman's face lit up and she ran over to me. Her husband had just retired, and they planned to go overseas in six months to visit one of their children. Could she have a mental goal to read books about the countries they would see? I barely replied, "That's a great idea," when she added, "I've been told people walk a lot over there. I could have a physical goal to walk every day before we leave so I'll be in shape . . . And, oh! I've been wanting to learn to sew, and I was just given a sewing machine. I could have a personal goal to take sewing lessons and make a dress for the trip." She caught the picture and was turned on to goals. What excited her most was seeing how they all worked together.

There may be times when your goals will dovetail just as clearly. But they don't need to in order to be consistent. Regardless of their practical relationship, your goals should, above all, enhance one another philosophically. They will do that if they contribute to your overall effectiveness. But they should never compete for your attention.

6. A goal must be dynamic.

If ever the saying applied, this is the time: Don't put all your eggs in one basket.

Goals, as we've already emphasized, are means to an end, not ends in themselves. Therefore, you might think of a goal as a continuous starting place, not a stopping point. Every goal is a potential springboard for future goals.

Several years ago I was in St. Paul, Minnesota, to teach a time-management seminar. I picked up the Sunday paper and saw an article about Dorothy Hamill, who became America's sweetheart when she won the Olympic gold medal for figure skating three years before. The reporter said, "A little more than a year ago, at least one sportswriter called her 'An American Tragedy.' " Then he quoted Dorothy herself: "I did go through a very bad time in my life. . . . There was a real letdown after the Olympics. I'd been working toward a single goal since I was a child. I achieved it at nineteen and I couldn't help but wonder what to do next. . . . I was depressed, confused. I ended up in the hospital with a bleeding ulcer within a year."[3]

Just two weeks later, I watched an interview with Diana Nyad following her record-setting eighty-nine-mile swim from the Bahamas to Florida. Her next goal was to swim from Cuba to Florida. The interviewer commented that one can only break so many records and swim so far. At what point would she have to quit setting such goals?

Diana responded energetically, "Oh, I do other things!" And she proceeded to tell of numerous interests and aspirations. She had already written two books, was writing a screenplay, studied Russian and hoped to visit Moscow someday and so on. Recently she popped up as a commentator for a televised sports event.

The number of things Diana does is not what is significant. You may never pursue in a lifetime what she achieved by her thirtieth birthday. But whatever you are working on, you should look beyond it.

Dynamic is defined as "tending to produce continuous change or advance." Goals keep you moving. The change may be in the same direction, or it may be down a different avenue altogether. What is important is that you are *open* to change. While some people quit an effort too soon, others hang on too long out of an overdeveloped sense of conscientiousness. Don't be ashamed to let go of a goal if you can't see it leading anywhere. One writer suggests we be cautious of new interests. They may be "false prophets." He cites the child who is forced to play the piano because she banged it enthusiastically as a baby, so her mother thinks she has great potential.

Give your inclinations a fair try; but don't be too proud to put them aside. With some goals, you will have no choice. A sudden change in your circumstances will automatically dictate a change. (That's why we have a purpose, remember? So we don't fall apart when our goals do.)

The opposite of dynamic is stagnant. Which sounds more appealing to you?

Entertainer Liberace told an interviewer, "If I've learned one thing in life, it's never feel like you've done it all."

"I dread success," wrote George Bernard Shaw. "To have succeeded is to have finished one's business on earth, like the male spider who is killed by the female the moment he has succeeded in his courtship. I like a state of continual becoming, with a goal in front and not behind."[4]

7. A goal must be desirable.

Several years ago a friend and I bought tickets to see the legendary play *Ramona* in a Southern California desert community. It is performed every spring with local talent in a natural outdoor setting. We trudged through dust and stones to get to and from the production and sat on hard bleachers under a blazing sun. As we walked back to the car, sticky and tired, I laughed and repeated what my mother used to say in similar circumstances: "If someone told me I *had* to do this, I'd feel abused."

How many times have you put up with discomfort and inconvenience to do something you *wanted* to do? Yet you've balked at less troublesome tasks? The difference lies in one word: *motivation.* If a goal passes all the foregoing criteria, and fails on this point, it fails altogether.

In the pages that follow we will look at eight goal areas. Given a soapbox, most people would express an opinion of how others should live in each category. Take the physical, for example. If you were to adopt everyone's cause, you would commit yourself wholeheartedly to jogging, jumping, running, aerobic dance, and weight lifting. You would eat brown rice, bran, and brewer's yeast. You would subscribe to a variety of vitamins and a vegetarian diet. While all of these have merit, in moderation, each individual must decide for herself what, and how much, will best enhance her health. In other words, whatever you choose, you must be committed to the principle, not coerced into the practice.

I worked with a man who had a twenty-five-year goal to memorize the Psalms. His plan included periods for review and allowed for breaks, as when he "got a little bogged down and decided to work on the Book of Colossians." At this writing he has fifteen years to go, and he says he thinks he'll make it. He wrote to me, "It has been rewarding and very worthwhile." While his goal requires a lot of concentration and effort, he has seen it as a pleasurable endeavor and a boon to his spiritual life.

On the other hand, I know of a fellow who is the product of a strict religious background and who for years mercilessly browbeat himself to memorize Scripture out of a sense of duty. It squelched his spiritual vitality and induced severe guilt, which ultimately required psychotherapy.

Goals are desires, not demands. A true goal incentive is not a guilt inducer. When you determine your goals, ask yourself, "Why?" If you answer with a "should," "must," or "have to," it probably won't motivate you for very long. We have enough mandates in our lives without having to create more.

One aspect of making a goal desirable is the way you word it. Your goals should always be stated *positively*. For example, rather than set a goal "to lose twenty pounds," you might make it "to weigh _____ pounds" (your ideal weight) or "to wear a size _____ dress." This may seem a small matter, but it is important in maintaining your motivation. Positively stated goals keep their appeal, whereas negatively worded goals come across punitively and eventually diminish your desire to achieve them.

If you have goals that meet all seven criteria, then you have a winning package. If you've never had a goal, the next chapter will get you started.

7

Determining
Goal Areas

On a television drama series a tethered single mother sighed, "I wish there were nine of me in the closet— one for my son, one for the office, one for a social life . . . But there's only one of me."

There's only one of any of us, so we can't give anything or anyone our undivided attention. But we *can* give *something* and get satisfaction from our efforts. And that is what goals accomplish.

It has been said, "No one plans to be mediocre; it just happens." No one intends to fail in a marriage, to incur poor health, to become financially strapped, to be a boring person, to get stuck in an ill-suited career. It just happens. But in many cases it doesn't have to.

I won't tell you that everyone must establish certain goals— there is no sacred system of goal setting. But I will suggest goal areas that describe functions most of us have in common and that deserve our attention. The categories are not exhaustive or exclusive, and should serve more as a model than a mandate. You may decide to follow this format, or combine one or more goal areas, or use different ones altogether. But for starters, let's consider four goal areas.

1. *Mental*—learning and thinking

Your brain is your most valuable asset and sets you above any other living creature. You have a remarkable capacity to reason, to reflect, to learn, to choose. Even if your IQ is closer to average than genius, you have an unlimited resource in your mind. Scientists maintain that we use but a small fraction of our mental powers in a lifetime. Barring physical damage or deterioration, you will never exhaust your intellectual capacity. You are more likely to waste it.

Mental goals keep your brain from collecting cobwebs and prevent atrophy of the gray matter. Mental goals answer the questions:

> *How will I use and expand my mind?*
> *How will I keep growing?*

I am fascinated by the art of thinking and am drawn to people who employ sound logic and rationale. Several years ago I met Dr. Charles Malik, professor emeritus of the American University of Beirut, and past president of the General Assembly of the United Nations. A brilliant scholar, he personifies intellectual prowess when he speaks. After hearing him make an address, I approached him and confessed I envied his brain. Since I knew a transplant was not an option, I went for second best and asked how he would advise someone to think. The crux of his response was to charge your mind with great literature and engage in provocative discussions.

Some time later I ran across a volume titled *I Love Books* and read the following:

> The first step toward becoming an original thinker is to become familiar with the thoughts of others. . . . The man who never learns how to read will never become much of a thinker. When left alone, his mind is empty because he has not filled it with useful knowledge and can make no comparisons of ideas. When cast upon his own resources, he finds no reservoirs of thought within him to refresh his soul. Wide reading is the very foun-

dation of ideas and constructive thinking, and the happiest person is the one who thinks the most interesting thoughts.[1]

I've thought of older people I know—men and women in their seventies, eighties, even nineties. Some are sharp and alert, others dull and lifeless. While numerous factors might be responsible, I know that my clear-witted, though perhaps physically feeble, friends are avid readers, always feeding their minds with fresh food. The less alert, by contrast, rarely pick up a book and seldom, if ever, challenge their own thinking. They are like the man whose epitaph read, "Died at 25; buried at 68."

Do you read profound books? Do you explore ideas in stimulating conversations? The man who wrote *I Love Books* said that books are no longer a luxury, but a necessity. Pulitzer Prize-winning author John Cheever lamented "the obsolescence of the intelligent reader."

Our twentieth-century motion madness threatens our cognitive growth. We may well become brain bankrupt if we keep moving in the fast lane. "Stopping to think," someone said, "is the first step in starting to think!"

If you don't know how to make the most of your mind, start by picking up a worthwhile book. Ask your librarian for a good reading list. Or ask well-read acquaintances what *they* read.

Later we will look at family goals, which at certain points touch other areas. For example, in *Honey for a Child's Heart*, Gladys Hunt brings books to life and builds a contagious case for exploring the world of words as a family. Her work is "must" reading for every parent. "Family closeness," she writes, "is not suddenly developed when children reach a certain age; it must begin from the first."[2] Reading together, she suggests, not only provides such an environment; it also builds "whole people" with "a valid world-life view."[3]

A headmaster with forty-one years' experience wrote in the introduction to Mrs. Hunt's book, "Few things are more important for a child than to discover the joy of reading. Give him a love of reading, and you have given him not only the most satisfying and useful of all recreations but also the key to true learning."

2. *Physical*—health and vitality

"Your body is your servant," says nutritionist Bernard Jensen, "It molds to the path you put it on."
Physical goals answer the questions:

> *How will I take care of my body?*
> *What healthful habits will I establish?*

This is a touchy subject. People can be quite defensive about how they tend to their physical well-being. Little wonder. Advice so proliferates on the topic that one is apt to rebel or just turn a deaf ear. Most of us are tired of hearing how we should live at every turn.

I attended a Toastmaster's Club speech competition to root for a close friend. One of the speakers was a young woman of very slight build who walked briskly to the rostrum in a sleek warm-up suit. She campaigned against the fitness fanatics and appealed to the audience to join her bandwagon.

"Look at me," she implored, "Do I look sick and out of shape?" She determined to stick to her preferred personal program of eating junk food, smoking cigarettes, and avoiding all exercise. She wasn't joking—I watched her empty a pack of cigarettes and polish off a plate of chocolate chip cookies in the course of the afternoon. Obviously she was a victim of overkill. But her reaction was unfortunately one of cutting off her nose to spite her face.

Dr. Hans A. Diehl, a postdoctoral research fellow in the study of coronary heart disease, says that "Americans have been brainwashed to believe they can live any way they want and then somewhere down the line, when they become ill, 'medics' will fix them up."[4] Dr. Jensen maintains that doctors make a living on our ignorance. Today's health trend substantiates his belief. It is common knowledge that traditional medical practices treated acute disorders and infectious diseases, all requiring the expert care and consultation of a physician. However, "today chronic illness makes up as much as 80 percent of all treatment. A recent study by the University of California—Los Angeles School of Public Health indicates that only 6 percent of all Americans are at a level of 'optimal wellness.' "[5]

People in the health and medical professions increasingly agree that the key to good health lies in the individual person. Norman Cousins heightened our awareness of the need to be totally involved in our own health and healing in *Anatomy of an Illness,* an autobiographical account of his partnership with his physician in overcoming a crippling disease. He wrote, "Studies show that up to 90 percent of patients who reach out for medical help are suffering from self-limiting disorders well within the range of the body's own healing powers."[6]

Along the same lines, psychiatrist Paul Tournier writes, "Many illnesses occur neither abruptly nor by chance, but rather have been prepared through years of a comportment contrary to the laws of life."[7]

Physical goals prompt you to consider the "laws of life" as they affect your health. Sensibility and moderation should be your guide. You don't have to join a crazy cult or subscribe to a ridiculous regimen. But you ought to do a little reading and research to determine what *you* need for optimum health.

At a national health convention, a lecturer told his audience that people die from shortages. Some people are short on exercise. Desk jobs and laborsaving devices reduce physical output, thus cheating bodies of wholesome exertion.

Others are short on nutrients, because the food they eat is less than nutritious. It is depleted of life-sustaining and life-promoting vitamins and minerals as a result of chemical adulteration. No longer can we assume that eating balanced meals from the basic food groups assures adequate nutrition. Nor is the notion acceptable that your body tells you what you need. Dr. Timothy Johnson, of the Harvard Medical School faculty, says that eating well can't be left to instinct; that "you really have to know something about good nutrition and act accordingly to end up eating a good diet."[8]

Another potential shortage not to be overlooked is rest. Ethel Renwick, who has spent a lifetime studying international diets and life-styles, writes, "One of the great ills of our society is that Americans make outrageous demands upon their bodies by overwork. The work ethic, being at the very core of America, is taken to an extreme and rationalized as worthy, even noble."[9] She particularly points the finger at Christians who "live as though God depended on them alone and had no other way of getting things done." While they wouldn't think of morally abusing their bodies, she says, they neglect what is "essential to physical soundness and growth." She poses a question that may lend some thought to your own physical status quo: "Some of us may have average health, but how many of us have exuberant health?"

One last thought on physical goals. I'd like to declare a moratorium on "dieting" as we know it. *Diet* comes from the Greek word meaning "way of life." Yet we have turned it to a woe of life. We have made it to be a crisis program, a crash intervention—anything but a desirable practice. As long as you jump from one fad diet to another, you will fail to achieve lasting benefits, and you'll end up chucking the whole effort altogether.

Whatever your beliefs about food and fitness, you would be wise to establish a way of life that pleases you and promises your body a healthy and consistent path to mold to. Remember, you can't pay for good health—you earn it.

3. Spiritual—faith and worship

A wealthy entrepreneur, speaking to a group of businessmen, put forth this query: "If you managed your financial life the way you manage your spiritual life, would you be bankrupt?"

Eugene Kennedy, professor of psychology at Loyola University wrote, "Learning to believe . . . goes along with growing up. The person who has not developed some belief system to

guide his life is probably not grown up in other areas as well.
... Believing is a problem for the theologian on a theoretical
level, but it is a practical one for all of us on an everyday level.
During the course of some research . . . I became aware of how
hard it is for most people to speak clearly about what they believe *in*. It is far simpler to describe what we believe *about*."[10]
Spiritual goals answer the questions:

> *What do I believe in?*
> *How will I practice my beliefs?*

Spiritual goals are as "practical" and "everyday" as any
other, if not more so, because they ultimately influence all that
we do. James Fowler, formerly on the faculty at Harvard Di-
vinity School, now director of the Center for Faith Development at Emory University, says, "We all need to make sense of
our lives . . . faith involves one's dynamic way of making
meaning."[11] "Faith makes life whole," wrote Helen Keller,
"and those who dwell in its Temple are happy because they are
whole."[12]
If this concept of wholeness—of meaning—sounds familiar,
it is because it is not unlike our discussion of purpose. In fact,
your sense of purpose quite naturally follows your spiritual
beliefs. If you had difficulty arriving at a purpose, it may be
that you haven't articulated your faith.
The Bible says, "The faith which you have, have as your
own conviction. . . ."[13] Someone commented that many convictions are family hand-me-downs. Hand-me-down convictions come when we accept answers without asking questions.
Dr. Kennedy praised the church that "permits man to be himself and to search. . . . The faith that makes man whole makes
room for questions and for the blessings of endless discovery
and surprise."[14] Probably the best in Christian thought has
come from the pens of those who doubted or questioned their
way to their beliefs.
Jesus asked his disciples, "Who do people say that I am?"
After hearing their various responses, he said, "But who do *you*
say that I am?" Deciding what you believe in—what you will

base your life on—requires that each of us answers that question.

But spiritual goals don't stop at your dialogue with God. Though this relationship is very personal, it is not private. It is something to share with like-minded people. Father Hesburgh, president of the University of Notre Dame, said, "People tend to think of faith vertically, but if you really believe in Christ ... you understand that the vertical dimension is only meaningful if it is expressed horizontally."[15]

This horizontal dimension is more than fellowship with others in a formal place. When I used the term "worship" to describe this goal area, I used it broadly. I might have said "service" or "good works" or "ministry." But some people are uncomfortable with these words because they can imply obligation or imperative.

I like to think that any outward expression of one's faith—be it teaching Sunday school, running a church nursery, knitting afghans for missionaries—is a form of worship because it is motivated by devotion, not duty. The rites and rituals of religion don't make a personal faith. In fact, they discourage and deplete it if they are ends in themselves. If there is to be any external exercise in the name of beliefs, there must first be an internal experience.

Before Saul the persecutor became Paul the Apostle, he met God in a vision on the road to Damascus. At once he said, "Who are Thou, Lord?" And then he said, "What shall I do?" In that order. Later, Paul would say of his ambitions, "The love of Christ leaves me no choice."[16] In other words, the motive of any ministry is the love of God, not the law of God. So, if we get sour in our service, it's a good sign we need to go back to the first question.

When you consider your spiritual goals, probably the most important criterion to apply is that they be "dynamic." So often people talk of their spiritual experience in the past tense. While your commitment in this area may have started with a particular event, it doesn't stop there. If you are saying the same things now about this dimension of your life that you were saying several years ago, chances are you are spiritually stagnant, and that you aren't enjoying "the blessings of endless discovery and surprise."

We have already looked at one example of how goal areas might be combined. Here is another. Spiritual goals partly concern horizontal relationships. So do social goals—our next subject.

4. Social—friends and fellow citizens

Social goals answer the questions:

> *What will I contribute to my community?*
> *How will I cultivate my friendships?*

At first consideration this goal area may set you on edge, adding to an already overwhelming range of relationships and responsibilities. But if you recall that one benefit of having goals is to deflect demands, you will understand why I have included this category.

Living in a democracy is a great privilege, but it also carries considerable pressure. We have infinite opportunities to contribute to the betterment of our country as well as that of other nations. And there's the rub. Who of us ever feels we have done enough—whether it is giving our money or our time to worthy endeavors? Some people, by nature or occupation, live in the mainstream of political affairs and social concerns. We must not let their involvement cause us to discredit our own contribution by comparison.

Good citizenship isn't limited to social activism and the role of consumer advocate. You don't have to wave a banner or pass out petitions to help humanity. I know some mothers who are up to their ears raising responsible children, and in doing so are contributing as much, and sometimes more, to society as their peers who are preoccupied with other critical causes. What is important is that you do what you can where you are and give yourself credit for that.

I write letters—both of concern and commendation. It's about all I can handle right now, but it gives me the satisfaction of contributing something to the good of others, if only in a small way. Our local newspaper printed my concerned editorial on the insensitive people I encountered in the undertaking business when I helped a friend arrange her husband's funeral. A cemetery director read it and called me to ask what he could do to prevent future recurrences. Then he thanked me for bringing the issue to his attention.

I especially like to praise persons and projects that make my life more pleasant. When I wrote to a reputable department store on behalf of a superior saleswoman, I received a reply saying my letter was the spur they needed to give her special recognition.

You may never spearhead a major movement or direct a demonstration. But you can do something. Let the normal flow of your life lead you.

Social goals not only call your attention to how you will live responsibly toward the "many" in your life, but they cause you to consider how you will closely relate to a few. I'm talking about friendships. Over a decade ago Alvin Toffler explored the impact on individuals of our superindustrialized society in *Future Shock* and devoted a chapter to interpersonal relationships. In the past, he noted, our relationships were tightly regimented and long lasting and generally confined to and dictated by our then limited human ties.

With increased mobility have come increased contacts. Social psychologists estimate a typical American's acquaintances to range from 500 to 2,500. Obviously intimate friendships with every one of those is impossible. But that isn't all bad, Toffler points out. Such "modular" relationships can be mutually satisfying and serve useful purposes. Contrary to those who decry such fragmentation, he states that total involvement with all our fellow men would clutter our psyches and create "an unthinkable mental condition."[17]

In the movie *Charade*, Audrey Hepburn initially snubs Cary Grant, telling him, "I have too many friends already. Unless one of them dies, I can't meet anyone else."

We would probably all agree that while some among us

sadly lack friends many face the opposite situation of knowing more people than we can effectively be committed to. This calls for an examination of expectations and a willingness to accept what Toffler calls "Monday-to-Friday friends" for what they are. At some point you have to decide just how involved you can be with those you know. It may seem a cold and calculating approach to friendship; but it is a kind one. Determining how much you can give to how many safeguards you from making promises you can't keep and letting people down.

Worse than overcommitment is the other extreme of distancing yourself from people to avoid intimacy and vulnerability. We all need closeness for our emotional health and growth. I heard someone observe that the divorce rate is as prevalent among single men and women as with couples. That is, the trend toward self-sufficiency has perpetuated an I-don't-need-anyone attitude, which encourages some to avoid commitment and avow independence.

Social goals should not coerce you into taking on the world and its problems. But they do call for a look at sustaining relationships and serving your fellow human beings.

I hope this discussion of four goal areas has stimulated you to contemplate your own goal areas. You may choose to define your goal areas quite differently, but the important thing is to begin thinking about them. We're only half-finished in our consideration of goal areas and will discuss four others in the next chapter.

8

More
Goal Areas
to Consider

There will be times in life when out of necessity or timeliness one goal area will take precedence over others. In fact, we will be discussing a little later the need and desirability of goal concentration. It is important, however, to look at all areas of your life when considering goals, lest you inadvertently shortchange an important sector. Sometimes, in fact, you might overlook something vital just because it is so close, so obvious, like your family. Here in this chapter, starting with home and family, we take a look at four more goal areas.

5. *Home*—family and furnishings

Home goals answer the questions:

What kind of atmosphere do I want in my home?
How will our family grow together?

At one time I titled this goal area "Family"; but I discovered that the single population bypassed it. If you are single, and without children, you have no less need to create a comfortable place to live.

Years ago I invited the wives of the men I worked with to my apartment for a brunch. One of them gazed around my kitchen in wonderment and said, "I didn't know single girls had nice dishes." She had married right out of high school and associated acquiring housewares with acquiring a husband. As absurd as her comment may sound, I know many single women who practice that philosophy. Their dwellings are carry-overs from college dormitory days, complete with orange crates and Snoopy glasses. The subtle message they are giving themselves is "I'm a girl until a man makes me a woman."

Your home—rented or owned—is an outlet for expressing yourself and should contribute to your wholeness and continuity. Begin to build a home before you are married, even if you are earning minimum wage and can purchase only one item each month or year. At least be working according to a plan.

Not surprisingly, it follows that many unmarrieds don't entertain. We'll talk a little about entertaining in chapter 14, but I want to mention it here too. Married or single, never let cramped quarters, meager funds, or sparse furniture stop you from having people over. Fellowship, not finery, is your objective. There's a Proverb that goes, "Better is a dish of vegetables where love is, than a fattened ox and hatred with it."[1]

The difference between a home and a house is the quality of life inside. While the decor lends a lot to the atmosphere, and should be part of your goal setting, your spirit ultimately sets the tone. What kind of home will you make?

If your home includes a husband and children, your goals should include your relationship to them. A counselor commented, "From the moment two people marry, they either grow together or apart." Tandem growth requires effort, contrary to the marry-the-right-person-and-live-happily-ever-after myth.

"Working at marriage," writes O. Dean Martin, "may mean planning or plotting. . . . Unfortunately, most of us don't like work. . . . But no such marriage exists that does not demand work and maturation. . . . For success in marriage you mustn't have a lottery mentality—putting in as little as possible, hoping to hit the jackpot. Instead, think of life as a solid investment from which you receive dividends in terms of what you put in. Work at care and maintenance. And, do it together."[2]

A few years ago the *U. S. News & World Report* devoted a special section to the American family, and concluded: "Indeed, the American family may be different—but it is far from dead. As one specialist puts it: 'I think people will think the family unit is an important one to maintain. It has something to do with their identity, practical reasons like support systems, and it can provide a richness to life.' "[3] The article stressed the importance of spending *time* together, particularly to set aside meals for communication. "People used to talk and listen at meal time," said Dr. Lee Salk, "but now they sit in front of their television sets with their dinner. I don't care how busy you are—you can take that time."[4] If you have never had a family goal, and the members of your household eat on the run, taking meals together is a good place to begin to promote family growth.

A marriage counselor says that a lot of families are like sand dunes—they are formed by influences, not purposes. What will form your home?

6. *Vocational*—skills and achievement

The dictionary defines *vocation* as: "a regular occupation or profession; especially, one for which one is specially suited or qualified; the function or career toward which one believes himself to be called."

Everyone has a vocation. Whether you go to a nine-to-five job, run your own business, or stay home with the kids, you have a "regular occupation," a "function" for which you are "specially suited." If you are a full-time homemaker, you, too, have a vocation. While you might think this section doesn't apply to you, it is no less relevant to your calling than to one that brings in a paycheck. I feel sad when I hear a woman say, "I'm just a housewife," because I think she must not be proud of what she does. The complexities and challenge of this career offer as many opportunities for growth and expertise as any other. They also require as much focus, because, as with any other pursuit, while you do many things, you can only master so much.

Vocational goals answer the questions:

> *What are my career aspirations?*
> *How will I attain them?*

A company recruiting management trainees headlined its advertisement, "You have a choice: A future . . . or a job!" Too many people let their job determine their future, rather than finding a job that fits the future they have designed. Of all the goal areas, this one puts the most noticeable dent in your time. So it stands to reason that it warrants careful planning. Yet experts say that, for many, if not most, this part of life is haphazard or hit-or-miss. Sadly, I've heard a career counselor say that 85 percent of people are not happy in their jobs. If such describes your job history to this point, take heart. The days of fixed careers are over. No longer do jobs require a till-retirement-do-us-part commitment. Career changes have not only become acceptable, they are expected. And both employees and employers are taking full advantage of this trend. The wise employee uses company goals to achieve his own; while the smart employer knows he gets the best work out of the most fulfilled people. That employer will encourage his people's personal pursuits, as long as they don't conflict with those of the company.

In *What Color Is Your Parachute?* Richard Bolles offers a manual for job seekers and career changers. After the problem of unemployment in our country, he believes the most serious situation is *under*employment—people "in the wrong field, at the wrong job, or well below the peak of [their] abilities."[5] He attributes this in large part to individuals not knowing what they want and assuming employers will put them in the right place. But the most important factor in your job happiness, he says, is self-initiative. Even career counselors, while helpful in fine tuning your options, cannot cut out your career path. Nor will circumstances create your ideal niche. You may envy successful people for their "lucky breaks"; but whatever they had going for them, they ultimately made their mark by a lot of self-determination and hard work.

Bolles maintains that you can just about write your own ticket if you are willing to plan, plot, and persevere. His three keys to success are:

1. You must decide just exactly what you want to do.
2. You must decide just exactly where you want to do it.
3. You must research the organizations that interest you at great length, and then approach the one individual in each organization who has the power to hire you for the job that you have decided you want to do.[6]

This advice is most useful for those who have had enough work experience under their belt to know their interests and aptitude. If you are more of a fledgling, the three keys given by another career counselor in a television interview might help you more:

1. Learn about yourself.
2. Learn what's out there.
3. Learn the skills for getting a job.

Central to all of these considerations is knowing your strong points. I have stressed the importance of emphasizing your strengths rather than your weaknesses when you set goals. This is particularly crucial to job success and satisfaction. If you don't capitalize on your good points, you won't convince anyone to employ you or your services. The director of a program that helps women reenter the labor force says, "There are many cultural myths and practicalities that we try to help women overcome so that they will be ready for jobs. One stereotype is that it is unfeminine to talk about your accomplishments, which puts women at a big disadvantage in job interviews."[7]

Career consultants all advise that you do your homework. But they also agree that, in the final analysis, you should trust your instincts. Further, you should not be unduly swayed by the trends. As someone cracked, if Elvis Presley had looked at job openings for musicians, he would never have become a singer!

7. *Financial*—sharing, spending, and saving

I know a lot of people who don't like to talk about money. They become uneasy, begin to fidget, and turn to other topics. Or they take the occasion to tell of its bad aspects. If ever the Bible was misquoted and misunderstood, it is on this subject. How often have you heard, "Money is the root of all evil"? But Scripture doesn't say that. It says, "The *love* of money is the root of all evil."[8] Inordinate attention to financial matters is wrong; but *inadequate* attention to finances can be worse.

Numerous writers on money management point out that the Bible has written more about money than any other subject—and on the importance of handling it wisely. I have read or skimmed numerous books on financial planning, and each related examples of clients whose irresponsibility with finances created havoc in their lives, including divorce and bankruptcy. The irony here is that ignoring money matters will, in the end, produce the very problem you tried to avoid. When poor planning puts you in a financial bind, money—or lack of it—takes center stage and absorbs your attention.

Financial advisor Venita Van Caspel observes, "The money game is not like any other game. You cannot choose whether you'll play. . . . Since you have no choice but to play, it behooves you to learn to play the game very well, for losing could mean spending your life in a state of frustrating, devastating financial insecurity."[9] She lists six reasons why people fail to become financially secure and end up financially strapped. One of them is "failure to establish a goal."

Financial goals answer the questions:

> *How will I manage my present resources?*
> *How will I prepare for the future?*

Speaking to church-oriented people, the president of a management firm says, "We have been taught much about giving, but little about how to faithfully handle all our money."[10] I think this is due, in great part, to bad theology. Jesus said we should not be anxious about our life and its physical needs. Some take that to mean not preparing for the future. But a minister clarified this command for me and said the principle is this: Live fretless, but not thoughtless, lives. Jesus himself taught numerous parables on the wise investing of one's resources.

At the same time, I don't subscribe to the increasingly popular notion that reduces God to a benevolent benefactor who indulges our material whims and grants us the Midas touch. The focus of financial goals is faithfulness and foresight with what we have, not frivolous acquiring of what we don't.

Venita Van Caspel says, "If you are a woman, don't ever think it is your inalienable right that a man should take care of your financial security. The single state—whether it is through choice, circumstances, death, or divorce—will probably be your lot for at least a part or all of your life. Even if you marry, you have an obligation to be a financial partner to your husband and to be as well informed as you can about money."[11]

Financial planning has little to do with financial plenty. I know wealthy folks who live irresponsibly from paycheck to paycheck, while others less prosperous keep money in the bank. I also know people who have limited means but are more materialistically minded than millionaires. Financial planning is for the purpose of controlling your money—so it doesn't control you.

Whatever your present financial situation—independent wage earner or dependent on another—you can make a difference in your present welfare and your future good by knowing what to do with a dollar.

8. Personal—hobbies and pleasure

Interviewed by *Working Woman* magazine, a marketing executive said, "I think women have always been intimidated by personal goals, or they feel that it's too masculine or too selfish to ask, 'What is my plan for me as a person? What am I about and where am I going?' ... If a woman who is sitting at home with two children says she can't make plans about her life until the children grow up, I say she's on the wrong track. It's called the 'wait until' syndrome."[12] Her point in the article is not that all women should be in the workplace; rather, that each should pursue satisfying outlets at every stage of life.

I met an ambitious single woman who worked her way up to manager of a reputable restaurant. She was one of only two women in the national chain to reach that position and was understandably proud of her achievement. She told me, "I've given all my energies to the company. Now I'm going to relax a little and take up a hobby or something. I guess I'll be self-centered for a while." I corrected her: "self-attentive." She hesitated, then smiled and said, "That does sound better."

Personal goals make sure you will be self-attentive. They answer the questions:

> *How will I express myself?*
> *What will I do for diversion?*

Ironically, you are more likely to be self-centered *without* a personal goal. If you don't have some kind of relief from the rigors and responsibilities of life, you will consciously or unconsciously resent everything and everyone that consumes your time. "A martyr," wrote Amy Vanderbilt years ago, "is never a warm and comfortable woman. . . . Whatever duty you have to your children and your husband, the household and the community, your duty to yourself as a woman must come first. . . . If you arrange time for yourself, you will be a better wife, a more contributing member of the community."[13] She adds a challenge in the form of a question: "Do you give yourself as much time off as you'd give the maid?"

Anne Morrow Lindbergh, whose reflections on coping with pressures we looked at earlier, holds the conviction that every woman "must consciously encourage those pursuits which oppose the centrifugal forces of today. . . . It can be physical or intellectual or artistic, any creative life proceeding from oneself. It need not be an enormous project or a great work. But it should be something of one's own."[14]

According to a physician, chronic fatigue is the most com-

mon complaint heard by doctors today. And while it could be
the first sign of a serious illness, or a subtle symptom of depression, it is often due to "energy imbalance: too much out
and too little in." He advises that "to stay physically and men-
tally vigorous, you must give as much time and thought to your
energy balance sheet as you do to your household budget."[15]
Earlier I told of a woman who took up piano again after many
years. When she had accomplished her short-range goals, she
said to me, "It's been so satisfying; I'm more inwardly calm."

"Doing what makes you feel good about yourself is really
the opposite of self-indulgence," say the authors of *How to Be
Your Own Best Friend.* "It doesn't mean gratifying an isolated
part of you; it means satisfying your whole self, and this includes the feelings and ties and responsibilities you have to
others, too. Self-indulgence means satisfying the smallest part
of you, and that only temporarily. It does mean being self-centered enough to care for yourself and to take care of yourself. If
you don't learn how to do that, you can never care properly for
others."[16]

I heard someone speak on "parent burnout," and he concluded by saying, "Pay attention to the first law of nature—
self-preservation."

If you can't think of any hobbies or special interests to take
up, call your local adult education office or a nearby college
and find out what classes they offer to the community. Sign up
for something you've never given much thought—music appreciation, upholstering, a foreign language, short-story writing. You just may find a hidden talent. I saw an inspiring
pottery demonstration by a man who was pursuing a career in
journalism. Years previously a friend asked him to take an evening pottery class with her, and he says his initial reaction was,
"I have articles to write for the newspaper. I've got to be out
gathering news." But he decided to go, and ended up teaching
pottery to college art students.

Another avenue for personal expression may be in one of the
eighteen thousand associations in our country. These groups
enlist people of like mind—or mania, in some cases—to share

favorite pastimes. Whether you love Porsches or poodles, astronomy or archeology, you can probably find kindred spirits somewhere in or near your locale. Check with the *Encyclopedia of Associations* in your library.

Personal goals foster self-preservation. Do something for yourself and you will do something for others, because when you are replenished you have more to give.

What Next?

By now you may feel like the baby chick depicted on a poster. The little creature has just pecked its way through the shell, and appearing somewhat stunned, exclaims, "Now what do I do?"

What you *don't* do is try to tackle all eight goal areas at once. This goal smorgasbord isn't meant to give you indigestion, but to offer choices to take one at a time. The next chapter explains how to strive for goals without straining in the process.

9

Putting Your Goals in a Framework of Time

If you have come to see the potential benefits in goal setting and have been giving thought to goal areas, it is quite possible that various ideas are floating somewhat aimlessly around in your mind. It's time, then, to get back to point number one of our requirements for setting achievable goals: A goal must be written.

I suggest that you make a horizontal chart like the one on page 117. This will give you a time line on which to figure your goals, using the principles that follow.

Long-range Goals

Long-range goals are *lifetime aims.* These are *less specific* than the mid-range and short-range goals, because they are less tangible. In other words, the closer you are to an objective, the more clearly you can see its details. You can't anticipate what you will be doing twenty, thirty, or forty years from now as accurately as you can foresee the next twelve months. But you *can* assume an outlook that will predispose you to certain choices along the way.

A long-range goal expresses the *overall style of life* you want

111

to attain. It is really a minipurpose statement. As you determine these lifelong aims, you should ask yourself:

> *How do I want to live?*
> *What will it take to satisfy me?*

Since your goals are an extension of your purpose, it is beneficial to visualize them in that way. To help you understand this concept, here are my own long-range goals arranged on a "mind map." I will explain this format in chapter 11, but for now the example is all you need to do your own long-range goals. (Though my own life purpose is not shown, you should write yours in the center space.) I keep this mind map in my personal planning notebook and review it every day so I keep sight of the whole picture.

To help you understand this concept, here are my own long-range goals:

Keep in mind that goals are a very individual matter and that these are merely examples of one person's outlook. Most goals are neutral. That is, they are not inherently good

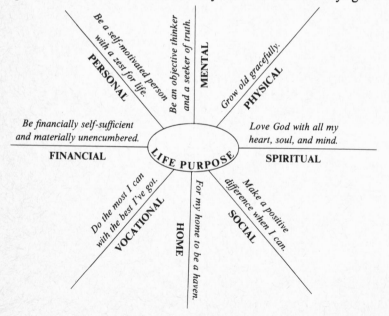

or bad. So avoid the temptation to comply with, compare to, or criticize others' goals, based on an arbitrary value judgment.

Mid-range Goals

Your mid-range goals are *projected accomplishments*. Here, you determine what you want to achieve as far ahead as you can see. That may be twenty-five years, ten years, five years, or five months—whatever you are comfortable with. The questions to ask as you establish mid-range goals are:

What motivates me more than anything else?
Does it honor my long-range aim?

Mid-range goals other women have set are: to open an IRA; to buy a home; to invent and market a game; to organize a gourmet dinner club; to learn a foreign language; to build a greenhouse; to finish the Boston Marathon; to go on a cruise; to start a preschool; to get a college degree; to increase self-confidence by completing a reading program and taking assertiveness training. These are just some of the limitless possibilities.

When you determine your own mid-range goals, throw caution to the wind and put down whatever comes to mind. You can fine tune your list later. Also, don't get hung up on the details of accomplishing a goal. If you stop to wonder how and if you will ever do it, you'll back off before you even write it down. Neither should you strain to think up goals just for the sake of having them. If nothing particular comes to mind in one goal area, leave it blank and go on to another.

When you have written all the possibilities, circle one or two mid-range goals to start to work on. Your choice will depend mainly on three factors: desire, circumstances (favorable and unfavorable), and need. You may be thinking, "But I want to do *all* of them!" Of course you do; that's why you wrote them down. But while all your goals may be tempting, they aren't all timely. By that I mean you can't effectively pay attention to every one at the same time. Here's a good place to practice the principle of separating the good from the best. I'll elaborate on this point later in the chapter, when I address goal concentration. But now we move on to how to make your mid-range goals happen.

Short-range Goals

Short-range goals are *present actions*. This is where the rubber meets the road. When you set a short-range goal, you determine the steps you must take to realize your mid-range goals. You answer the questions:

> *What must I do first?*
> *What must I do next?*

Short-range goals get you started and keep you going.

In any goal area, you will usually have more short-range goals than mid-range goals, and more mid-range goals than long-range goals. You might liken a long-range goal to a forest, the mid-range goals to the trees, and the short-range goals to the branches. The closer you are to achieving a goal, the more details you deal with.

For example, my long-range vocational goal is to "do the most I can with the best I've got." At the present time I am pursuing two mid-range goals: to write a book, and to be self-employed teaching seminars. When I established the goal to write a book and asked, "What must I do first?" I decided I should write an article to find out if I had what it takes to write a whole volume. When I accomplished that, I asked, "What must I do next?" Some of the short-range goals that answered that question were: to outline the book, to contact publishers, to research material, and so on. At the same time I determined short-range goals for my seminar enterprise: to take an accounting course, research the market, design two new seminars, send a mailing to prospective clients, set up an office in my home, and more.

While setting short-range goals naturally follows setting mid-range and long-range goals, it isn't initially necessary to determine them in that order. If you are new to goal setting, you may, in the beginning, have immediate goals in mind without a future context. That's fine—go ahead and accomplish those. They will either become dead-end streets, or they will lead to longer-range desires.

It is not necessary to have a clear goal sequence for each goal area—that is, a long-range aim complete with mid-range and short-range activities. Your main objective is not to fill in all the blanks on your goal chart immediately, but to organize what desires you do have and to open your thinking to areas you've not before considered. If you write down only one goal, you have made a good start. Accomplishing goals will naturally generate new ones.

Years go I had a general desire to do some public speaking, so I set a goal to schedule two engagements in the next year. I ended up speaking more than twice and began to specialize in a few topics. One was time management. That led to writing a seminar, which led to teaching more seminars, which led to writing a book, and so on. One goal leads to another, and to another, and to another.

Shown on page 117 is a simple goal-setting chart you can make on an 8½" by 11" piece of paper. Remember your purpose in using this chart is not to fill in every space, but to have a place to put the goals you already have in mind. Note the boxes designated "Priority" and "Timetable." If you have more than one goal on your chart, you must make a choice (*see* "Goal Concentration" on p. 116). And once you make a choice, you must make a commitment to trying to achieve it by a certain date. Under "Timetable," write the target date for completion and the date by which you should begin it. I suggest that you come back and fill in these two categories after you have read the planning chapters, where I discuss these principles in more detail.

Goal setting lets you dabble in several things before you define a few. Trial and error is part of the goal process. It works in five stages:

1. Experiment   (You explore several possibilities.)
   ↓
2. Enjoy   (You learn what you like most.)
   ↓
3. Excel   (You learn what you do best.)
   ↓
4. Eliminate   (You shed less-satisfying endeavors.)
   ↓
5. Emphasize   (You determine your focus.)

No goal is so fixed that you can't change it. Most people switch horses midstream at least once while accomplishing a goal. This is normal, and it is healthy—unless, of course, the person is a goal hopper who never sticks with anything. For the conscientious goal achiever, major changes are as much a part of success as what remains unaltered. I don't see changes as mistakes; I see them as an important part of any achievement. How will you know if you don't try? In the trying, you learn more about what you want and what you don't, what works and what doesn't. You have that much more information to work with when you plan more goals in the future. Just as you can't steer a parked car, you can't very well direct your life unless you are moving toward something.

Goal Concentration

A common error made by goal setters is to tackle too much too soon. It is far more important that you accomplish one objective effectively than to spread yourself so thin that you make no real progress in any area. Often your present situation dictates the goal you will concentrate on.

When my health became a major problem, thus a top priority, my interest in nutrition grew. I set a goal to have an all-natural kitchen, meaning I would eliminate refined and processed foods and would prepare meals from pure and fresh ingredients whenever possible. Initially, I spent an inordinate amount of time planning menus, arranging my kitchen for optimum functioning, reading a wide variety of nutrition books,

GOAL WORKSHEET

GOAL AREA	LONG-RANGE	MID-RANGE	SHORT-RANGE	PRIORITY	TIMETABLE
MENTAL					
PHYSICAL					
SPIRITUAL					
SOCIAL					
HOME					
VOCATIONAL					
FINANCIAL					
PERSONAL					

and experimenting with recipes and food combinations. For the first month I cleared major chunks of my evenings and weekends for this undertaking and even turned down social engagements that involved eating away from home. Some might have thought me to be fanatical. Rather, I was intensely *focused* for a time. I knew it would pay off in the long run, and it did.

Goal concentration establishes consistent habit patterns. Erratic commitment, on the other hand, keeps you from being effective in any area. Good nutrition is such a way of life for me now, that it is second nature. I think nothing of making mayonnaise and dressings, preparing dried legumes instead of buying canned products, sprouting seeds, juicing vegetables, grinding grains, and baking breads. There are people who look at me and say, "I don't have time for that," which is what I have said to my friends who refinish furniture. What we are really saying is, "That is not one of my priorities." Because it really is true that we make time for what we want to do.

Goal concentration also produces significant accomplishments that might not otherwise happen. If you were to read biographies of accomplished people, or talk to a number of them personally, you would find a common strand to their success: their ability to do one thing at a time, to put the most important goal in front of other activities.

I already mentioned that the goal you select to work on should lend itself to your immediate situation. If several do that, you must make a choice. Here's where people get into trouble. They feel guilty if they put one goal first, as though they were favoring one child over another. If you put some goals on hold, you are simply saying, "This is important to me, but now is not the most advantageous time to work on it." You are actually honoring that goal by waiting until you can give it your best. And just because you are focusing on one goal area does not necessarily mean you are ignoring the other dimensions of your life. It just means you don't tackle new or major tasks in other areas until you get where you want to be in one.

On the radio I heard Dr. James Dobson tell of the period

when he was earning his doctorate in psychology. He and his wife became aware that they weren't communicating as well as they might. While their marriage was not particularly in trouble, they wanted to prevent a potential problem. So he took a year off from graduate school to concentrate on their relationship. Of course he did other things, and probably even continued a certain amount of independent studying. But he determined to *focus on the family,* which, interestingly, is now the name of his broadcast.

If you feel lopsided because of a forced or chosen emphasis at a particular stage in your life, consider it an investment in the future. This is why a goal worksheet and, particularly, long-range aims are helpful. They keep the whole picture before you so you won't feel fragmented just because you are focused.

It's Never Too Late

It's never too late to have a goal. At any stage of life, a goal provides tremendous satisfaction. I read about an eighty-five-year-old great grandmother who graduated from college—sixty-six years after she finished high school! In her commencement address she urged the graduates to "have a plan with a definite goal . . . a reason for getting up in the morning." She told an interviewer that her new goal was an expedition to Africa. I was reminded of some lines I ran across in a card shop:

> If you have a goal in life
> That takes a lot of energy
> That requires a lot of work
> That incurs a great deal of interest
> And that is a challenge to you
> You will always look
> Forward to waking up
> To see what the new day brings.

Embrace a goal and you will enhance your life.

PART THREE

How Do You Plan the Use of Your Time?

*Dost thou love life? Then do not squander Time;
for that's the stuff Life is made of.*
BENJAMIN FRANKLIN

10

Planning: Straitjacket
or Life Preserver?

"I only plan my time when I have to," said a woman attending one of my time-management seminars. I was curious, so I asked, "When is that?" "When I get under the pile," she answered.

The purpose of planning is to *prevent* you from getting under the pile, not to bail you out when you're in too deep. Here, especially, an ounce of prevention is definitely worth a pound of cure.

But most people avoid planning like the plague. If you are among this majority, this chapter will help you examine your notions about this essential part of managing your life. First, we'll look at the barriers you may be putting up, and then we'll list the benefits you may be missing. I sometimes use the words *planning* and *scheduling* interchangeably, though planning is a broader concept than actual scheduling. Each, however, presupposes the other.

Barriers to Planning

Here are four reasons why people don't plan their time:

1. They don't believe in it.

There's an old tale about a man who put a tightrope over the Grand Canyon and walked across it. Then he asked the crowd that had gathered if they thought he could go over pushing a wheelbarrow. They all said yes and applauded as he accomplished the second feat. Next he asked, "Do you believe I can do it with someone *in* the wheelbarrow?" Again, everyone yelled cheers of support—until he asked for a volunteer. Of course, no one climbed in.

I have yet to meet anyone who did not agree that time management—in particular, planning—is important and necessary. But as soon as I offer a way, they back down. Why the retreat? Because they aren't convinced it will make a difference in their lives. As with dieting, they may have tried it now and then, but haven't stuck with it long enough to see results.

A speaker delivered a dynamic talk and concluded by saying, "I don't want you to believe one thing I've said . . . I want you to go home and do it." The believing comes in the doing. If you really believe planning will better your life, you will do it. If you don't, you won't. You must agree not only in principle, but in practice. You must get in the wheelbarrow!

2. They don't see the problem.

I was referred to the vice-president of a university by one of his colleagues and arranged to see him to discuss the possibility of doing a time-management workshop for his staff. He received me graciously but explained that they had everything under control.

Long ago I learned that one does not win friends and influence people by telling them they are wrong! But I was so baffled by this man's blind spots that I went against my better judgment and mentioned that I had to call his office more than fifteen times (I lost count) before I finally reached him. Unflinching, he justified his case for five full minutes . . . and I rested mine.

Had this person established a simple system with his secretary, my time and hers would have been saved. We could have reduced all those calls to two—the first to find out when he preferred to take my call, and the second to return it. His comment was that he didn't have a set time to be in the office or to talk on the phone because he wanted to be available to his staff whenever they needed him. What he didn't understand was that by being available to everyone, he was available to no one—because not even his secretary ever knew where to find him.

3. They don't want to change.

Unlike the university vice-president, many people are apt to see the problem; however, they are less apt to see it as *their* problem. They resist change because they think it is the *other* person who needs to change. We will discuss this aspect when we look at the first benefit of planning, which is the principle of being in control.

But there is another reason why people don't want to change: They don't want to cramp their style. What they don't realize is that their style is cramping them. "Free spirits" fear loss of their freedom. To them, a schedule is no different than a straitjacket. But the truth of the matter is, without one they are usually in a bind of their own making. One of my closest friends, a convert from this way of thinking, describes her transformation:

> I was the least likely person for time management, because I'm the creative, spontaneous type, and creative people are usually afraid of getting organized. But I became fascinated with the idea that I could get things done.
> Procrastination was a cloud that hung over me. I was like an overeater: Left to themselves, overeaters will overeat. Procrastinators who are left to themselves will do everything but what they're supposed to do.
> I had never sat down and followed any kind of plan. I just wanted to keep moving to the next exciting thing. So I constantly put off doing the hard tasks, and then I had to face the consequences. People got mad at me because I didn't keep my word; and I couldn't sleep at night because all this stuff kept running around in my head.
> When I learned how to follow a plan, things got under

control. Now I have *more* freedom throughout the day. And for once I can say no, which frees me to say yes later to what I really want to do. People even like me better—someone told me I am a very valuable person because I'm creative *and* organized. I was always passed by when important jobs were handed out; now I've even surprised myself by being given a responsible management position.

In this day and age people are kidding themselves if they think they can live spontaneously. They will live with unbalanced checkbooks, unwritten letters, unanswered phone calls, broken appointments . . . and guilt.

Without some kind of structure in your life, you are doomed to disappointing others and, worse, to disappointing yourself. Changing is painful, but not nearly as painful as staying the way you are—if the way you are is robbing you of fulfillment.

4. They don't want to take the time.

This is a classic paradox—the belief that one cannot afford the time to plan. Dale Carnegie tells a story that illustrates the trap we fall into. A forest-products company hired a new logger. His first day on the job he broke all records and felled more trees than anyone ever had before in a single day. The second day he worked even harder, but he felled only three-fourths of the number of trees he brought down the previous day. On the third day he sweated and strained, and swung his ax more vigorously than ever, but he only downed one-half the trees he had on the first day. His foreman observed this and finally asked him when he had last sharpened his ax. The logger replied that he was too busy cutting trees to sharpen his ax.

Effective people take time to sharpen their ax. They know the truth of the principle that an hour spent in planning is worth three or four in execution. They have learned the difference between utilizing time and merely using it. Management consultant Merrill Douglass suggests that we would spend time quite differently if we had to buy it. Unlike any other resource, he says, "Time is free. All you need to do to receive your daily allotment of time is to wake up each morning. Because time is free, (we) don't value it very much."[1]

Time is also limited. This is another paradox: that few people have enough, yet everyone has all there is. Look at time as you would a fixed income. Make it enough because it is all you have. You won't come up short if you budget it wisely. The bottom line is, if you're too busy to plan, you're too busy.

Each of these barriers to planning is surmountable, given the motivation to overcome them. If you are not profiting from planning already, the following list of benefits will show you what you can anticipate if you plan your time. Peter Drucker says, "Time management takes perseverance and self-discipline, but no other investment pays higher dividends." When you plan, you reap dividends; when you don't, you may reap disaster. Here are your options.

Benefits of Planning

1. Control versus being controlled.

I addressed an association of hospital administrators and began by asking what, concerning time management, they wanted to learn during our session together. One by one, each person expressed a need or frustration. Then the personnel director of a major medical center said, "I want to find out what my bad habits are." At that I said, "Bless you! You are a wise man."

Successful people own up to their responsibility. They know that effective time management comes from effective self-management. A college senior told me he failed two classes because he had too many other priorities. When I asked him what those priorities were, he named several persons who vied for his attention. Since he didn't have a plan to answer to, he acquiesced to each and every interruption.

The difference between planning and not planning is the difference between a thermostat and a thermometer. A thermometer *registers* the temperature of the environment, whereas a thermostat *regulates* it. Likewise, individuals without a plan let

the people and pressures around them dictate how they operate, while persons with a plan operate according to their own
dictates. Keeping to a plan does not mean cutting off people.
But it does prevent you from capitulating to other people's
whims . . . and compromising your priorities.

Control is defined as "power to direct or regulate; ability to
use effectively." When you plan your time, *you* control it.
When you don't plan your time, you abdicate the controls. But
how can you control your time when powers beyond your control waste it?

Time wasters (anything that keeps you from accomplishing
your objectives) fall into two categories—external and internal.
External time wasters are generated by other people or outside
influences—such as traffic jams, broken equipment, and the
telephone. Internal time wasters are self-generated; they are
caused by you and are under your direct control.

If asked to list their greatest time wasters, most people will
reply with external time wasters. The majority of people either
do not recognize or are unwilling to admit that the majority of
their time wasters are really internal ones. In fact, at every
workshop I do, at least one person takes me to task and insists
it's a losing battle—that it doesn't matter what she does, because she still must contend with mismanaged, disorganized
people.

Beware the victim mentality. If you believe you are at the
mercy of others, that is exactly how you will operate. There are
plenty of people who would like to control your time, and they
will if you let them.

When you point your finger at external time wasters, you
lose control. Of course, sometimes they deserve it. Nothing is
more frustrating than to conscientiously plan your time, only
to have others set you back by missing deadlines, canceling
commitments, and forgetting promises. The truth is, there will
always be uncontrollable external influences. No amount of
planning will change your environment or the people in it. But
it will help you deal more successfully with them.

Consider the supplier who doesn't deliver your order on

time. He has clearly blown it. But you might not be "up a creek" had you anticipated that possibility and allowed more lead time in your planning. You can't possibly foresee every problem that will arise, but you can prevent a lot of chaos at your end by counting on crises and building a buffer into your schedule.

Further, many external factors are neutral—they are merely activated by your self-generated responses. What, for instance, would happen if you didn't answer the phone just once?

Following is a list of common internal time wasters. Note the cause-and-effect relationship most of them have to planning.

Procrastinating
Unrealistic expectations
Inability to say no
Clutter/personal disorganization
Lack of goals, priorities, or deadlines
Indecision
Daydreaming
Impulsiveness
Attempting too much at once
Rushing
Constantly switching priorities
Leaving tasks unfinished
Too much socializing
Ineffective communication
Making other people's decisions

Control of your time concerns not only *what* you do, but *how much* you do, and how you feel about it. Dr. Scott Peck wrote of an incident that occurred during his psychiatry residency training. He described a period when he began to resent his fellow residents because he was putting in so many more hours than they were. He went to the director of the clinic where he was assigned and explained his frustration. Mac, the director, acknowledged that Dr. Peck had a problem, but matter-of-factly told him that it was *his* problem with *his* time. Dr. Peck admits he hated Mac for three months because he was so callous. Then, he writes:

> I somehow came to see that Mac was right. ... My time was my responsibility. It was up to me and me alone to decide how I wanted to use and order my time. If I wanted to invest my time more heavily than my fellow residents in my work, then that was my choice, and the consequences of that choice were my responsibility. ... If I did not want to suffer them, then I was free to choose not to work so hard and to structure my time differently.... As it happened, I chose not to change my life-style. But with my change in attitude, my resentment of my fellow residents vanished. It simply no longer made any sense to resent them for having chosen a life-style different from mine when I was completely free to choose to be like them if I wanted to.

Then he concluded:

> By requesting Mac to assume responsibility for the structure of my time. ... I was giving him my power, my freedom. I was saying in effect, "take charge of me. You be the boss!" Whenever we seek to avoid the responsibility for our own behavior, we do so by attempting to give that responsibility to some other individual or organization or entity. But this means we then give away our power.[2]

Every day I meet people who have given away their power. An intelligent, well-educated woman just told me how exhausted and disconnected she feels because of a long list of commitments she has to fulfill in the next month. I'm afraid I wasn't very sympathetic because I have watched her live like this for years. I asked her why she took on so many responsibilities, and she replied, "I wanted to do all of them." She said yes to each request—and even initiated some—then felt sorry for herself. She was a victim of her own making. I have an idea *she* wouldn't like Mac very much either!

2. *Accomplishment versus activity*

A man once made news by assembling creative contraptions out of junk and rigging them to a motor. A passerby watched one of his works in motion and asked, "What does it do?" The inventor said, "Nothing, it just runs."

Do you have days when you just run? Sometimes you simply can't avoid it. But that should be the exception, never a way of life. You can busy yourself from sunup to sundown; but unless you have a plan, you may end up with nothing to show for your efforts—except a tired body. In *The Canterbury Tales,* Chaucer captured the barrenness of busyness in describing a person we have all seen (or been):

> Nowhere so busy a man
> as he there was,
> And yet he seemed
> busier than he was.

Perpetual motion doth not a time manager make. In fact, this trait is a dead giveaway of a poor manager of time. As Alec Mackenzie says, "Nothing is easier than being busy and nothing more difficult than being effective."[3] Successful time management is measured by the *results* you achieve, not by the efforts you expend.

We have all encountered the erratic driver who darts in and out of lanes only to arrive at a traffic light the same time we do. Some people go through life that way. I have already confessed to having been one of them. I favored the fast lane and spurned slow movers. Then I got a speeding ticket in the form of a physical breakdown and was forced over on the shoulder for over a year.

Initially I envied all who whizzed by me, and I longed to be back there with a heavy foot on the gas pedal. But as I studied the traffic, I saw the futility of rushing. I realized that the people who observed the speed limit and frequented the rest stops got much further in the end than those who tried to set a record. When I finally merged back onto the highway, I determined to stay close to the inside lane, with ready access to the exits. I still enjoy hard work, but not at a harried pace. Occasionally I revert to old habits, but I pay for it in engine trouble and poor mileage. And so will you, if you function in a frenzy.

But neither do I advocate poking along. I just don't say as much about it because the majority of women I know veer to the other extreme. However, I am well aware that out there are also sleepers, sometimes referred to as underachievers. Rather than dart from one thing to another, they just drift. But the outcome is the same—activity without a sense of accomplishment. Planning helps move this type of person out of hibernation. Occasionally someone makes my day at a seminar, saying, "I've been blessed with health and energy, but I'm wasting it. I want to take better advantage of my time and opportunities."

Whatever your style, you can regulate your pace through realistic planning. It may mean you cut back and do less, or gear up and do more. You will find a happy medium as you combine conscientiousness toward your time with consideration of your capacity (the topic of discussion in chapter 19).

"Most people don't think in terms of minutes," Alan Lakein writes. "They waste all the minutes. Nor do they think in terms of their whole life. They operate in the mid-range of hours or days. So they start over again every week and spend another chunk unrelated to their life-time goals. They are doing a random walk through life, *moving without getting anywhere*"[4] (emphasis added). Planning covers the bases, keeps you moving, *and* gets you somewhere. This is the difference between doing and getting things done.

3. Important versus immediate

Does this sound familiar?

Your husband has left for work and the children are off to school. It's time to get really moving on the day's routine. You go upstairs to make the beds, but when you get there, you decide to gather the laundry.

In your son's room you notice that his goldfish bowl needs cleaning, and you take it downstairs to the kitchen. Looking around for a newspaper to put under it, you realize there are definitely too many papers cluttering up the house. You decide to bundle them up and put them out for pick-up.

Once outside you see that there are dandelions coming up in your new lawn, and you stop to dig them out.

And so it goes. Before you know it the kids are home from school and the beds aren't made yet.

Who of us cannot identify with such a situation? Have you ever made so many stops between the kitchen and the bedroom that you forgot what you were originally after and had to retrace your steps? Such mindless meandering is not unlike putting out little brushfires while the homestead burns to the ground.

In a booklet titled *Tyranny of the Urgent,* and appropriately printed with a bright pink and orange cover, it states, "We live in constant tension between the urgent and the important. The problem is that the important task rarely must be done today, or even this week. ... But the urgent tasks call for instant action—endless demands pressure every hour and day."[5]

Planning protects against that pressure. When you plan, you determine your priorities and give them space on your schedule, knowing that if you don't, lesser matters will vie for your time—and likely get it. It is like making a hotel reservation. If you arrived at a hotel and learned that your room had been given to a "walk in," you would be out a place to stay, not to mention pretty upset. But how many times do you cancel commitments to yourself? You plan to accomplish something significant, but somehow it gets upstaged and goes undone.

Certainly there are those situations when interruptions are not only urgent, but are also important and need your attention—a family crisis, a friend in need, and so on. And there are unexpected occasions that call for sudden change or spontaneity—a spur-of-the-moment lunch date, an impromptu afternoon jaunt, a last-minute weekend excursion.

A schedule that precludes flexibility is well crammed, but not well planned. Wise planning allows for what I like to call being *selectively sidetracked,* while also accomplishing important and necessary tasks. I once heard this helpful distinction: "There need not be routine, but there must be regularity; there ought not to be mechanical stiffness, but there must be order; there may not be haste, but there must be no trifling with our own time or that of others."

In his army days, General Dwight Eisenhower said, "Urgent matters are seldom important, important matters are seldom urgent." Planning guards against confusing the two and keeps you on a productive and peaceful path.

4. Attention versus distraction

Have you ever been with someone who was somewhere else? By that I mean someone whose mind was on the next ten things he or she had to do. Or maybe you have been that person—wanting to give your undivided attention to someone or something, but distracted by pending projects. This happens when we feel squeezed by time constraints and anxious about getting everything done. Rare is the person who concentrates on the present.

I have said there are no easy answers to managing your time. But there is almost a little magic in following a plan. In a remarkable way, a plan alleviates a lot of anxiety. When you map out a strategy for the next day, week, month or year, you allow adequate time for your top priorities. So when you are involved in one activity, and another from your list pops into your mind, you can dismiss the latter one, knowing it has a "reservation" on your schedule.

In his best-selling book *Blue Highways,* college professor William Least Heat Moon chronicled his extended travels over the back roads of the United States alone in his small van.

Early in his experience he wrote of learning "to sit full in the moment" and of practicing the "awful difficulty of just paying attention." He observed that "any traveler who misses the journey misses about all he's going to get—that a man becomes his attentions."

If your attentions flit about, you shortchange yourself of precious time. You not only miss the meat of the moment, but you lose even more if you have to take a chunk of tomorrow's time to make up for today's distractions. And you create a steady cycle of robbing Peter to pay Paul, while seeming never to break even. Thus, frustration, not fulfillment, characterizes many a day's end.

Psychiatrist David Burns observes that when we distract ourselves from the task at hand by obsessing about endless other things we haven't gotten around to doing yet, we get in a bind and overwhelm ourselves into doing nothing. "To illustrate how irrational this is," he explains, "imagine that every time you sat down to eat, you thought about all the food you would have to eat during your lifetime. Just imagine for a moment that all piled up in front of you are tons of meat, vegetables, ice cream, and thousands of gallons of fluids! And you have to eat every bit of this food before you die! Now, suppose that before every meal you said to yourself, 'This meal is just a drop in the bucket. How can I ever get all that food eaten? There's just no point in eating one pitiful hamburger tonight.' You'd feel so nauseated and overwhelmed your appetite would vanish and your stomach would turn into a knot. When you think about all the things you are putting off, you do this very same thing without being aware of it."[6]

Planning puts an end to this paralyzing pattern so you can "sit full in the moment" on your journey through life.

I know a man who carries enormous responsibilities, but he never appears weighed down, and he never cheats a person or project of his full attention. He is a conscientious executive and a committed friend to many. Early in our acquaintance, I wrote the following in my journal:

Today I sat with one
　　who knows
　　the gift of time,
Gratefully he receives it,
Generously he shares it.
He takes time to ponder, to wonder, to muse;
He gives time to inquire, to listen, to care.
He hurries not,
　　but accomplishes much;
He values minutes,
　　but does not clutch them;
He plans his day,
　　but does not protect it.
He brings about a sense of timelessness
　　in a world of morbid clock-consciousness.

I have heard this friend say, "Time is limited, but it is adequate for all we're to do. Having a schedule that makes sense comes from knowing what we are supposed to do, doing it, and no more."*

It must have been a practitioner of planning who said, "People don't need to add years to their life; they need to add life to their years." Planning adds life to your years.

* Since I completed writing this book, this friend has become my husband—and my greatest mentor in the art of effective living.

11

How to
Make Plans
You Can Follow

At the heart of planning is the art of anticipating. When you plan, you employ foresight to estimate what you will accomplish in a particular period of time. You determine your objectives based on whatever information you have at the moment concerning the future.

To use the phrase "plan ahead" is redundant. You can't plan "behindhand"; you can only plan beforehand. This explains why the woman who said she only plans her time when she gets under the pile is usually under the pile. To resort to planning for remedial action is to miss its intended benefit of anticipatory action.

The adage "Plan your work, work your plan" suggests two laws of successful scheduling:

1. A schedule must serve a broader plan.
2. A schedule must serve *you.*

This chapter is devoted to principles and practices that bring about both, providing you keep in mind and apply the concepts covered previously. Planning and scheduling deal with the "when" of your life, but to be effective they must take into

account the "who," the "why," the "how," and, "how much."
Certain precepts are basic to any planning you do. Refer occasionally to those listed here, to insure that your plans meet
these standards.

Planning Precepts

1. Commitment

A halfhearted effort at planning will yield less than desirable
results. Commitment comes from the conviction that this is
something you *want* to do in order to live how you want to live.
A commitment to planning is a commitment to yourself.

2. Consistency

Plan regularly. Make planning part of your routine rather
than an afterthought.

3. Completeness

Cover all bases when you plan. Respect details, because they
will either deliver you or do you in. Planning need not be
complicated, but it must be thorough.

4. Clarity

Ambiguous language is a time waster. State in simple and
concise terms what you want to accomplish. Clarify the action
you will take, the results you want to achieve, and the deadlines you must meet.

5. Capacity

Set limits. Think *optimum* capacity, not full capacity. Sitting
at your desk with a blank schedule and a long list of things to
do is like standing at a plentiful buffet with an empty stomach.
The temptation in both situations is to put too much on your
plate. And the outcome in each case is that, if you do, you will
regret it. Don't overschedule *or* underschedule your time.
Build reasonable flexibility into your plans.

6. Concentration

Do one thing at a time. Stick to what you begin until it is completed. Concentrate on the most significant efforts necessary to accomplish your objective. Do what is necessary and no more. The Pareto Principle, also called the 80/20 Law, holds that a "vital few" activities (20 percent) usually produce the major results (80 percent). Don't expend effort on the "trivial many" activities (80 percent) where the remaining results (20 percent) will not be noticed.

7. Consolidation

Cluster activities on your schedule. Group tasks homogeneously—by function (phone calls, correspondence), geographically (errands), by priority (*A, B, C*), or chronologically (for a succession of time commitments).

8. Cooperation

Let other people help you. Exchange responsibilities with friends, colleagues, children, spouse, and others. Beware the disposition to indispensability. In the workplace (and even home), agree to a common "quiet hour" for planned unavailability and uninterrupted concentration.

Planning Procedures

The procedure of planning requires that you mind your *P*s: Patterns, Projects, Priorities, and Pace. In this chapter we'll discuss Patterns and Projects.

Patterns Keep Momentum Going

If you want to be an effective time manager, begin by establishing effective habit patterns. Another word for this is *routine*. Routine keeps a good momentum going and provides a kind of rhythm to your life. Because you don't have to concentrate on routine activities, you can apply that mental energy to more important things.

The Value of a Routine

While routine is automatic and predictable, it should never become tedious or regimented. Routine should accommodate you, not vice versa. A schedule that is a sacred cow ceases to serve its purpose. Also, routine should feel comfortable, never controlling or confining. If it becomes monotonous, inconvenient, or inefficient, change it. Do not be legalistically locked into a system.

Learn to distinguish between healthy habit patterns and unhealthy patterns. Good habits save time; poor habits waste it. If a certain routine detracts from your purpose, or delays your doing a high-priority activity, you should eliminate or change it. An example of this is spending an inordinate amount of time straightening your desk in the morning (make it part of your routine to do it at night), or lingering over coffee and the newspaper during your prime functioning time. Such habits accommodate procrastination and divert you from your goals.

Dr. Merrill Douglass suggests five steps "to improve your effort to eliminate self-defeating habits and replace them with self-reinforcing habits":

1. Identify the habit you want to change.
2. Carefully define the new habit you wish to develop.
3. Begin the new behavior as strongly as possible.
4. Never deviate from the behavior until the new habit is firmly established.
5. Use every opportunity to practice the new behavior.[1]

Some routine is regular but infrequent. Be sure to include it in your long-term planning. For example, when you wash the curtains, note on your calendar the next time they should be done, so when that month or week rolls around it will already be scheduled. Otherwise, you will likely forget about it until you are serving dinner to a guest and look up in embarrassment at dirty drapes.

Long-term projecting keeps routine current and serves to stagger big tasks so everything doesn't pile up on you at inopportune times. When your schedule shows a commitment to one of these routine tasks, you are less apt to put it off saying, "One of these days I'll get to it." Then, by the time you do, it often requires more work, or conflicts with another priority. For instance, the week before Christmas may not be the best time to notice your windows need washing!

Short-lived routine is very effective and can offer a refreshing change of pace. If you want to complete a particular project, for example, establish a new and temporary pattern for your evenings. It may work out like this: Arrive home, sort and read mail, jog, fix a simple dinner, socialize for a set period of time, or read a select portion of the paper, then work on your project until bedtime. If you are a morning person, you might get up two or three hours earlier than usual (which also means making sure you retire at a reasonable time). If you are *not* a morning person, you ought to consider becoming one. It *is* possible to change (I know, I'm a convert), and well worth it. Most people find they can accomplish as much in the quiet of two early morning hours as they would need four to six hours for during the day when interruptions, distractions, and noise are greater. This is especially true for mothers who have little or no time to themselves in the evening.

I know a couple who are starting their own business while the husband holds a full-time job. They get up at four o'clock, while the children are still sleeping, and work until seven, when he gets ready for the office. They figure it will take a year to get it off the ground, and they are willing to pay the price.

The Planning Process

Part of your pattern should include the actual activity of planning. You have probably heard it said that if you fail to plan, you are planning to fail. Managing your time is like maintaining a good relationship. When things go smoothly, you are apt to forget it is because you have worked at it. Once you start thinking you can get by on instinct alone, you will become lax in your efforts, and you will sacrifice success. Planning works for you when you work at it.

Long-term plans cover any period of time beyond a month. Decide on a planning period that is comfortable for you, and allow ample lead time to feel adequately prepared. I like to plan quarterly, or seasonally. So I set aside four blocks of time each year to plan for the next three months. For example, I plan in August for September through November, in November for December through February, and so on. I do that at least two weeks before the quarter begins.

For a number of years I missed my sister-in-law's September 2 birthday, because I didn't think about September until September 1—and then it was too late to mail a card. By planning in mid-August, I have plenty of time to send a greeting. In fact, I buy all my greeting cards at once for each quarter and put them in my tickler file (see chapter 17).

Once a year I like to take a day or two to get away and really think long-term. I reflect on where I have come from, review my goals, reevaluate my priorities, and refresh my broader sense of purpose. I have a friend whose supportive husband watches the children and sends her to a nice hotel for a weekend so she can get her wits together. Later they go away together and mesh their mutual plans.

Immediate plans cover time frames less than a month— usually a week or day. As with long-term plans, you should do immediate planning before the day or week is on top of you. Always plan the night before for the following day. You will sleep better and wake up calmer. A little preparation today saves a lot of panic tomorrow.

Both long-term and immediate plans are necessary to effective time management. Long-term plans lead into immediate plans but do not dictate them. Sometimes immediate priorities will preempt long-term ones. This does not discount your long-term plans. In fact, it makes them that much more necessary, because they provide a point of reference from which to deviate and to which to return. Otherwise, you have no basis to distinguish the urgent activities from the important ones, and will risk succumbing to a mode of urgency.

Projects Reduce the Feeling of Fragmentation.

One of the most common frustrations concerning time is the chronic feeling of being overwhelmed. "To do" lists multiply like rabbits and are ever-present reminders that you aren't getting it all done. Worse, they create the feeling that you are out of control.

The goal of planning is not to get everything done, but to do the *most important* things. *Project* planning identifies those important activities and reduces the feeling of fragmentation that lengthy lists of random tasks provoke. When you feel fragmented, you can't concentrate; when you can't concentrate, you can't focus; when you can't focus, you can't get anything done. Project planning helps you feel calm, focused, and productive in the midst of a myriad of demands on your time.

A friend showed me her depressing list of things to do shortly after she and her family moved to a new home. She was behind in everything before she began to do anything. We looked at her list together and realized that the majority of tasks hanging over her head could all be consolidated under one project called "house settling." She mapped a project and immediately felt relief. Now she could take one thing at a time, over a reasonable period, and have a sense of accomplishment every day even though there was a lot left to do.

Think projects when you plan. A project is any task or activity that has three or more steps. Each project you plan should have five ingredients: Statements, Scheme, Steps, Schedule, and Sources.

The *Statements* summarize the purpose and goal(s) of the project (the why and what).

The *Scheme* diagrams your undertaking from start to finish.

The *Steps* derive from the scheme and detail all the items you will do to complete the project.

The *Schedule* targets due dates for each step.

The *Sources* list every resource (person, money, thing) necessary to the success of the project.

Mind-Mapping

Research on the activity of our brain provides helpful insight for effective project planning, particularly the diagram portion. Scientists tell us that we actually have two brains rather than one, and each deals with very different mental activity. The left, or academic, side of our brain, deals with language, logic, numbers, and analysis. The right, or more creative, side, deals with rhythm and music, imagination, dimension, color, and daydreaming. Both are essential to maximizing our potential.

Tony Buzan, in his book *Use Both Sides of Your Brain,* explains that our traditional training and education encourages left-brain functions to the sacrifice of right-brain performance. For example, we learn to think, outline, summarize, and plan in linear sequences. This requires that we organize our ideas in our heads before we even put them down, thus stifling the flow and freedom of our creative abilities.

Buzan advocates mind-mapping as a start to overcoming lopsided brain functioning and combining synergistically the capacity of both sides. A mind map is a pattern of connected ideas linked to each other around a main theme. Mind maps can branch into as simple or complex a structure as you desire. In fact, an interesting side note here concerns dramatic results attained with slow students who were exposed to this process. Grammar-school children who were judged as having learning disabilities and who showed almost total lack of understanding in certain subject areas confounded teachers with brilliant explanations of the same subject when they applied the principles of mind-mapping.

For the purpose of planning, mind-mapping is usually very simple, though you are free to take it to any extent. On page 145 is an example of a project I mind-mapped.

Mind maps take the tedium out of planning and make it more than palatable. People continually tell me that once they have learned this method, they develop a more positive attitude toward planning. Mind-mapping is an excellent way to start your children managing their time. Kids enjoy drawing

Project: Garage Sale
Today's date: 4/10   Target date: 5/12

(Statements)
  Purpose: Clean out clutter
  Goals: Free up closet and drawer space;
          Make extra money for fall wardrobe

(Scheme)

(Steps)

Do:	By:
Clear garage	4/15
Kitchen cupboards	4/18
BR closets	4/20
BR drawers	4/24
Guest room	4/26
LR chests & bookcases	4/30
Bthrm. cupboards	5/6
Place news. ads	5/10
Make signs	5/8
Label merchandise	5/9
Set up tables	5/10 & 11

(Sources)

Errands/Shopping:	Delegate:
Buy tags	Jane — ads
Extra cash	Ruth — cash box

* Buzan advises that all words on a mind map be printed in capitals for optimum clarity.

145

creative maps of their own goals and responsibilities and, parents tell me, more eagerly carry them out. As a family, make a mind map together for your next vacation. Get out the colored pencils and draw pictures on the branches to depict your plans—an airplane and tickets, suitcases, palm trees, ice-cream cones, and so forth. Determine the steps, schedule, and sources (don't forget the budget!); then assign each family member certain responsibilities toward the preparation.

Tackling a project is like eating an elephant. Do you know how to eat an elephant? A bite at a time! Breaking down a project into steps gives you bite-size pieces you can handle. One of the major causes of procrastination is trying to do tasks that are too big. Paralysis sets in when you see all that has to be done and you think, *How will I ever do this?* Anytime you face that situation try to reduce the task to smaller segments of activity.

When I began to write this book, I quickly learned that authors don't simply sit down and produce a manuscript. They write sentences and paragraphs and chapters. They knuckle down at the typewriter and knock out reams of pages, many of which end up in the wastebasket. They reword, revamp, rewrite. On tedious days, when nothing comes, they are tempted to toss the whole thing.

I knew my book was an elephant, so I mapped out the "bites" by chapters. When the chapters became elephants, I broke those down into sections. On many occasions I got so stuck on a section that I separated it according to subpoints. I needed to do that so I would keep at it and see progress. Step-by-step perseverance keeps your goal or project within reach. Remember, inch by inch, it's a cinch!

Some projects are so large in scope that it is helpful initially to make a mind map showing the overview, then to do a separate mind map for each area. A student in one of my classes did that for her goal of starting a private psychotherapy practice. Days later she told me she felt more excited about the prospect of her new career and was already accomplishing more toward making it happen.

Ahead of the Game

When you schedule the steps of a project—or when you schedule any activity, add a 20 percent buffer to each task. Unrealistic time estimates (one of the most common internal time wasters) will get you in trouble. Travel time to and from destinations is a major culprit. Most people schedule travel time as though they expected every light to be green, no one else to be on the road, and a parking place awaiting them when they arrive. And then they wonder why they are always in a rush and running late.

If the 20 percent buffer does not work for you, determine your own buffer zone. A secretary at her wit's end told me that everything her boss gave her took twice as long as she estimated. It never occurred to her to compensate at the front end by giving him an estimate double her expectations. He always asked her how much time she needed, and then he counted on that. Her constant state of pressure was self-inflicted, as are many problems people face in the use of their time.

Even if *your* estimates are realistic, others' may not be; and most of what you do ultimately involves someone else. If you beat a deadline, you are that much better off. It is a lot easier to *use* extra time than to *create* it.

Speaking of deadlines, add a buffer to those as well. If a report is due on Friday, June 12, plan to have it completed by Wednesday, June 10. Some things have to be done at the last minute, but not nearly as many as the average person saves till then. Take the report, for example. Even if you have to wait for input from someone else, or for information only available at the eleventh hour, you can still complete everything but the final details.

Get in the habit of being ahead of the game, in small tasks as well as large. In fact, especially in small things, because they make a big difference. Do you lay out your clothes the night before, or do you pull things out of the closet in a panic minutes before you are to leave for work—and then find out a button is missing? Do you buy your traveler's checks one to two weeks before your trip while you are already out doing errands, or do you race to the bank just before closing on the eve of your vacation?

If you are a last-minute person, you have a self-defeating habit that should be changed into a self-reinforcing habit. You are not hurting only yourself, but everyone else in the path of your tailspin. Few people recognize that this kind of pattern is basically selfish because it puts others on the spot. It isn't fair that someone who conscientiously keeps commitments should continually suffer because someone else doesn't.

Determining a Schedule

When steps of a project follow each other sequentially, you determine the schedule by beginning at the target date (i.e., realistic deadline) and working backward, just as you do when you determine what time the Thanksgiving turkey should go into the oven. In my example of planning a garage sale, only the last few steps depended on a linear sequence. The others could have occurred in any order, but I arbitrarily selected deadlines for each one so I wouldn't have too much to do the week of the sale.

While some projects themselves actually determine the amount of time you need, and therefore the amount of time to allow on your schedule, in the case of others, the amount of time you *have* determines how much you can spend. For example, if you are enrolled in an evening class and you also hold a full-time job, your time for studying is limited. In such a situation, apply the "time and amount" principle. Say, "This is how much time I have to prepare for tomorrow's class. I can spend a half-hour on each chapter and no more." Then, in the time allotted, enforce the 80/20 Law mentioned earlier, and concentrate on the efforts that will accomplish the most effective results. Think "time and amount" for any activity that is "never done"—cleaning or preparing a speech, for example.

Sources of Help

When you determine the Sources your project will need, remember the precept of cooperation. Part of wise planning is learning to delegate. Before you put anything on your schedule, be sure you're the one who has to do it. A good time manager entrusts responsibilities to someone else whenever possible.

Swap errands with a friend, let your child put the green stamps in the redemption books, have an assistant take notes for you at a meeting you cannot get to. Delegation is not abdication. If someone takes a task off your hands, you are still responsible. Don't breathe down the person's neck; but give ample instructions at the outset, and at some point make sure it gets done.

If you delegate to your children—apart from their normal chores—be sure to respect *their* plans and privacy as you want them to respect yours. A friend of mine demonstrates this by having her children make their own weekly schedule. If she wants their help, they look at their schedules together and arrange a suitable time. She never takes them for granted, and they don't resent her requests.

When I taught the fourth grade, I was impressed by the harmonious home one of my students came from—particularly since she was one of seven children. She told me one day, "If my mom is out doing something for our family—like buying groceries or taking someone to the doctor—our part is to watch the younger kids. But if she goes out for fun with my dad or a friend, she pays us to baby-sit." Wise parents!

List every kind of material or product you will need in the course of working on your project. Have you experienced the frustration of starting something, such as hanging pictures, only to realize that you don't have enough hooks? You could have picked them up a number of times when you were out, but now you have to make a special trip to the store. The waste of time, energy, and car expense is obvious. Practical foresight, which is what planning is all about, minimizes last-minute frenzy.

Last in the consideration of Sources is the budget. Here is straightforward advice from the Bible:

For which one of you, when he wants to build a tower, does not first sit down and calculate the cost, to see if he has enough to complete it? Otherwise, when he has laid a foundation, and is not able to finish, all who observe it begin to ridicule him, saying, "This man began to build and was not able to finish."[2]

You do want to be able to finish what you start. And now that you've learned to establish productive patterns and set up manageable projects, are you sure you're doing the right thing at the right time? To give you that assurance, we'll go on to prioritizing and pacing next.

12

Determining Priorities and Setting Your Pace

Establishing a smooth-flowing pattern and mapping out projects with skill are essential planning procedures and may make us quite efficient—but for that effectiveness we are looking for and the assurance that our plans advance our life purpose, we must learn two more procedures: how to establish priorities and find our own pace.

Setting Priorities Aids Effectiveness

Setting priorities—giving precedence to the most important objectives—sets apart successful people from the rest of the population.

The annals of management history will long tell the account of Charles Schwab and Ivy Lee, because it supports the significance of prioritizing. When Schwab was president of Bethlehem Steel he challenged Lee, a consultant, to "Show me a way to get more things done with my time and I'll pay you any fee within reason."

Lee handed Schwab a piece of paper and told him to write down the most important tasks he had to do the next day and to number them in order of importance. He instructed him to begin at Number One as soon as he arrived at work the next morning, and to stay with it until he completed it. Then he was to recheck his priorities and start in on Number Two. He added that if any task took all day, not to worry about it. Stick with it, he said, as long as it remains the most important.

Lee told Schwab that when this method worked for him, he should give it to his men. Then he could send him a check for what he thought it was worth. Some time later Schwab sent Lee a check for $25,000 (a sizable sun in the early 1900s!), and later attributed turning Bethlehem Steel Corporation into the biggest independent steel producer in the world to Lee's advice.[1]

First things first! That's what priorities are all about. What's good enough for a multimillion-dollar corporation is good enough for you. The decisions you make may not have widespread financial consequences, but they are every bit as strategic to the success of *your* operations. In his book *Thought Vibrations* Victor Segno points out, "Many people scatter their plans over too large a field, and while they are competent to do great things, if done systematically and in order, they fail because they never come to a decision as to just what they are going to do first."[2]

How to Set Priorities

Most time-management manuals tell you to prioritize your activities into *"A," "B,"* and *"C"* categories (*A* for most important to *C* for least important), and you are left to decide arbitrarily which is which. Before you determine the *order* of priorities, however, it is helpful to determine their *nature*. Here is a way to distinguish the kind of activities you are dealing with:

A priorities *advance* your goals and other projects. They return the greatest benefit to you over time and produce maximum results for your long-range objectives (write a resumé, redecorate a room, research what computer to buy, for example).

B priorities *back up* the *A* priorities, or long-term plans.

They are the day-to-day, week-to-week, month-to-month maintenance tasks that are necessary for basic survival (grocery shopping, laundry, and so forth) or for stability in ongoing operations (bookkeeping, phone calls).

"C" priorities are *"could dos"* that contribute to your sense of accomplishment or enjoyment, but have no real relationship to *A* and *B* priorities. These are random, short-term tasks that are nice to do but are not necessary, such as reorganizing recipe files, having lunch with a casual acquaintance, and so forth.

You will spend *most* of your time on *B* priorities. But you should spend your *best* time on *A* priorities. Schedule at least one *A* priority each day, and schedule it as early in the day as possible—during your peak performance time. Likewise, schedule the most difficult part of a project early in the week. When you do the hardest task first, the rest of the day or week goes more easily.

Once you group your priorities, you can determine their order of importance. Simply number each task in your *A* and *B* categories: *A*-1, *A*-2, *A*-3, *B*-1, *B*-2, *B*-3. (*C* priorities are generally not scheduled, but arbitrarily chosen to fill free time as it comes up. Those are the occasions you can pick the one you *feel* like doing.)

If you can't decide which task should be Number One and which should be Number Two, ask, "Which will produce the maximum benefit?" If you still can't make a choice, ask, "Which will cause the greatest *consequences* if it is *not* done?"

Working With Your Priorities

Ask these same questions when a conflict of priorities arises between you and a boss, colleague, or spouse. Here is where communication is so important. Many individuals compromise a priority in bitter silence, assuming the other person is deliberately balking them, when in reality that person may be totally unaware of the situation. This works both ways: You may, on hearing the other side, realize that your priority is of lesser immediate importance. Most people respond to reason. Adhere to the art of "win-win" negotiation, which means looking for a resolve that serves the best interests of both parties (as opposed to win-lose, or lose-lose).

Forcing yourself to number your priorities keeps you from putting them off. Some people procrastinate on the harder things on their lists because they are afraid of them. They are particularly afraid of the *A* priorities because they usually have not done them before, and they don't know what to expect. Further, because they are part of longer-range objectives, they seldom see immediate results of their efforts. So they gravitate to *B* priorities that are predictable, or *C* priorities that are enjoyable, because both give a sense of accomplishment. Actually, what they give is a *false* sense of accomplishment. Over the long run greater satisfaction comes from accomplishing *A* priorities.

Another kind of person may fearlessly pursue *A* priorities (because they are new and exciting) and let the necessary basics (the *B*s) slide. The important thing is to adequately tend to both *A* and *B* priorities.

State your priority activities using action verbs. "The proper use of words can motivate you to do the task and actually assign a relative priority to the task. For example, write 'Call Mr. Smith,' instead of 'Mr. Smith.' Action verbs are very important. They denote an action is required on your part to complete the task."[3] Here is an example list of action verbs that describe typical tasks:[4]

Call	Work on
Write	Submit
Prepare	Change
Develop	Send
Go to	Add
Make	Talk to
Meet	Pick up
Review	Deliver
Check	Get
Determine	

Daily Activities

Prioritize your daily activities each day. That may sound obvious, but what I am saying is that you cannot know more than one day at a time what is most important. Though you have a plan, circumstances may require you to veer from it and tend to more urgent matters.

So, each day reevaluate your priority list and reestablish your *A*-1, *B*-1, and so forth. Don't even list any *C*s because just seeing them there, wanting to do them, and knowing you probably won't, will frustrate you. Keep your *C* list somewhere else so you can get to it when you have time for it, but it won't get to you when you don't. (In chapter 17 I will talk about how to set up a system to keep all this information in one place.)

Your daily priorities specify *what* you want to accomplish, but need not specify *when*—except for appointments and meetings or major projects you want to save a large block of time for. It is not so important that you designate an *exact* time to do a task, but that you allow *enough* time. It is okay to say, "From two to three in the afternoon I will write three letters"—if you are fairly certain that period of time will be open. But if baby Billy is fussy at two o'clock, your objective will be frustrated. Instead, put "write three letters" on your schedule, and anticipate that during the course of the day an hour, or snatches of time adding up to an hour, will be available to write your letters.

Do not despair if large chunks of time are not at your disposal. You can be just as productive using free moments as free hours, and maybe even more so because you have to make them count. Don't minimize the value of minutes and fritter them away while you hold out for hours to tackle a task. When ten minutes come your way, write the first sentence of that proposal you've been meaning to send to the new company that moved into town.

This is why it is so important to work from a priority list, because when you suddenly have free time, you don't use half of it trying to figure out what to do. How often when those unexpected breaks pop up, do you thumb through a dog-eared magazine or stare at the wall? There is nothing wrong with that either, if it is what you really want to do. The point is, if you want to relax and do nothing, do it on purpose so you can fully appreciate it and not feel guilty. Otherwise, accomplish something and save up those would-be wasted times so you will have a larger block of time to play with during an evening or weekend.

Think about what you can do with little bits of time that become available during the day. The following ideas just tap the possibilities.

What you can do in 5 minutes
Sweep the kitchen floor
Write a postcard
Fill the saltshaker
Read an article
Sew on a button
Scrub some potatoes
Make a phone call
Do sit-ups or jumping jacks
Scour a pan
Hand wash a dress
Pick out next day's outfit
Wrap a present

What you can do in 15 minutes
Mop a floor
Write a letter
Water the plants
Read a chapter of a book
Dust the furniture
Make a grocery list
Put new photos in an album
Mend a torn seam or knit a few rows
File paperwork
Polish shoes
Brush the dog
Iron a couple of outfits

What you can do in 30 minutes
Clean out the refrigerator
Straighten a closet
Update your address book
Plan a party menu
Hem a skirt
Take a long walk
Write in your journal
Play a game with your children
Water the garden
Polish a silver piece
Make an original birthday card
Give yourself a facial and take a catnap

Such minijobs will vary from person to person, but you can see how much potential there is in a small portion of time and how, little by little, you can accomplish a lot.

Alan Lakein points out that however well you plan and prioritize, there will always be minute-to-minute decisions you have to make. When that happens, he advocates asking Lakein's Question, which is, "What is the best use of my time right now?" If your answer is "I don't know," he says, keep asking the question because "if you really don't know the best use of your time, then there's nothing more important than finding out."[5]

When you can come to the end of a day feeling more satisfied over one thing you accomplished than dissatisfied over ten things you didn't, you will know that you are an effective time manager.

Pacing Gives a Feeling of Well-Being

Pacing is the most difficult aspect of planning to master, because it requires regulating both the number of activities you attempt and the rate at which you accomplish them. But pacing is essential to a feeling of well-being as you go about your day, and helps to keep you in the calm eye of the hurricane.

Four words sum up what I want to say about pacing: *Brisk, Breaks, Enough, Flexibility.*

Brisk.   In the book *Getting Things Done,* Edwin C. Bliss relates a management consultant's observation that the "tempo" of a company contributes most to corporate success, yet "is something to which most executives and corporate bodies remain blissfully indifferent." Bliss elaborates:

> Tempo is a reflection of the attitude of the person in charge. If that person is goal-oriented ("Now that we know exactly what our objective is, let's do whatever has to be done to get there"), the pace is brisk. If that person is procedure-oriented ("Let's make sure we follow directives to the letter, and don't risk any mistakes"), the pace is sluggish.
>
> At a person level, the same thing is true. If you are dawdling, drifting, and *working at* a task instead of *doing* it, blow the whistle on yourself.[6]

Brisk does not mean fast; it is not a function of speed or rapidity, but of the vim and vigor with which you approach things. The dictionary defines *brisk* as "lively" and "energetic." Briskness will look different on everyone, but try to find that pace for yourself that is a little faster than comfortable.

Breaks.   A friend studying psychology tells me that no one can effectively concentrate more than fifty minutes at one sitting. When you work on a task that requires a lot of concentration, you will work more effectively if you leave it for brief intervals. Take a minute to stretch, get a glass of water, make a phone call—something you can do and then get right back on track. Simple *B* priorities provide good breaks from *A* priorities. And when you've really worked hard and want to reward yourself, do something from your *C* list.

Just as you need these periodic breaks throughout the day, so you need relief from longer stretches of concentrated effort. For example, there were times I put the writing of this book aside for the weekend or for an entire week, and even a month. I needed to get away from it, and you will need to get away from some things too. Self-discipline has two sides: knowing when to keep at something, and knowing when to let up.

Enough.   In the field of economics there is a principle called the law of diminishing returns. It states that after a certain point, profits or productivity do not increase in proportion to further investment of resources. Then, capital and people are used unwisely.

Likewise, we hit points in our own lives when we don't get a comparable return on our efforts. Most often this occurs when we overexpend our internal resources, when we go way beyond what is necessary and pace ourselves poorly. Such occasions are not only unproductive, but can also become *counter*productive. Living effectively is knowing when that extra effort and those additional hours make a difference, and when they don't. Usually they don't. In simple English, know when you've done enough!

Edwin Bliss gives three questions to ask yourself as a safeguard against doing more than enough. His questions provide a practical companion to the Pareto Principle (the 80/20 Law).

1. Exactly why am I trying to do this task? Is it really worthwhile? If so—
2. Have I set a deadline for myself? Have I resolved to meet it?
3. If my life depended upon doing the task in half the time I have allocated, what shortcuts would I take? Is there really any reason *not* to take them?[7]

Heed Parkinson's Law: Work expands to fill the time available!

Flexibility.   When your child needs help with his homework do you reluctantly put aside your own paperwork? When your boss asks you at eleven o'clock to take a client to lunch at noon, do you bristle? These are legitimate interruptions. You can either tolerate them (resenting the intrusion) or take them in stride (accepting them as normal).

In chapter 10 we discussed the importance of controlling your time and counteracting interruptions. Am I now saying the opposite? No, both principles are equally true. Some interruptions are reasonable, some are not. Here one must invoke the "Prayer of Serenity" and seek the "wisdom to know the difference."

A secretary once said to me, exasperated, "I could get more work done if it weren't for the telephone." Sometimes we lose sight of the fact that interruptions are often an integral part of our jobs—and therefore of high priority. So I pointed out to her, "The phone *is* your work." A few weeks later she told me she saw her job in a completely new light and had even begun to take pride in her phone skills.

In order to properly pace your activities, you must have a fairly realistic estimate of who and what rightfully requires your time and how much you can expect to be "on call." If you anticipate that unexpected demands will take four of your eight working hours, then don't optimistically put six hours worth of priorities on your schedule. You will only feel increasingly agitated toward "intruders" and fail to concentrate well on any task.

This issue always causes a "red light to go on" when I speak to health-care professionals. They say, "We aren't like anyone else, because our job is all emergencies and crises." I agree; but the same principle of planning holds for them as for computer programmers: Know how much time you can call your own and how much you can't.

At a recent workshop a head nurse with pressures and responsibilities beyond what most of us ever experience moaned, "I'm lucky to accomplish one thing every day." So I said, "Then you should have only one priority on your schedule for tomorrow." She stared at me, first in disbelief, then in sudden relief.

Banish the belief that doing more is doing better, and schedule only what you can realistically handle. Don't fill your schedule like you pack your car trunk for a trip. Think of your schedule as a floor plan. A pleasing floor plan is never cluttered or crowded. Likewise your schedule should have plenty of breathing space and the freedom to move things around. Your purpose is not to see how much you can put into a planning period; your purpose is to sensibly order your life. The person who accomplishes eight tasks in a day is not necessarily better managed than the individual who finishes only one. The key to pacing is to anticipate how much of your time you can control and allowing for what you can't. This takes practice and patience.

A schedule is like a computer—it only prints out what you put in. If yours tells you to do too much, it is merely following your orders. Change your input and it will change its readout. Remember, it is there to serve you, not to bully you.

I once happened on a terrific belated thank-you card. It said, "My slowness in expressing my sincere thanks was caused by a circumstance genuinely beyond my control. . . . My calendar broke."

Sometimes your calendar will "break" and your plans will fall apart. How to fix them is the subject of the next chapter.

13

What to Do About Planning Problems

Have you heard of Murphy? He's the one who writes all those laws. Here are three:

"Nothing is as simple as it seems."

"Everything takes longer than you think."

"If anything can go wrong, it will."

When you make plans, you anticipate that one or all of Murphy's laws will come to pass. I call it being optimistically pessimistic. Part of being a good planner is being a good adapter. Plans aren't exactly made to be broken; but they *will* be, for any number of reasons. As Robert Burns poetized, "The best-laid schemes of mice an' men gang aft agley."

After you put together a plan—short-term or long-term—you scrutinize it and ask, "Will it work?" Anyone can design a fancy schedule; but a *functional* one is another matter. Be tough on yourself. You may have a plan you *want* to work; but if you are realistic, you may have to admit the likelihood that it won't. Change it before you charge in.

On the other hand, your plan may be sensible and workable. But midway through, something or someone throws a wrench into the works. What do you do? You can always panic; but that's a terrible waste of time. Better to call time and think things through. Whether you have problems before you launch into a plan, or encounter them later on, you can remedy the situation by employing one of four actions.

Solving Planning Problems

1. Rearrange your timetable. Ask, "Is there a better time?"

Arranging your priorities on a calendar is quite like laying out a dress pattern. You wouldn't start to cut the fabric until all the pieces are in place. Sometimes they fit well the first try. When they don't, you shuffle them around until each one has enough room.

When two or more priorities crowd each other, the solution may be as simple as shifting them to different times on your schedule. (Reminder: Use a pencil!)

One of my three-month plans involved a considerable amount of business travel. Since I was flying through Dallas, I scheduled a week of vacation at the end to visit family and friends. Though my plans looked good on the calendar, they didn't set right with me. I realized that I needed to be back at the office that last week to get ready for some important meetings. At first I thought I would have to forego the vacation. But after closer consideration I saw that I could schedule it *before* my other trips. Though it seems an obvious solution now, I was slow in seeing it, because I naturally think of relaxing *after* I work. But it turned out to be a good switch.

Sometimes the "better time" is in a later planning period altogether. Be open to all possibilities. So often when people plan, they get stuck on one time frame and sacrifice more expedient ones—which nearly happened to me on the above trip. It is also human nature to get stuck on certain *ways* of doing things, which leads to the second solution.

2. Replan your priorities. Ask, "Is there another way?"

Suppose when you lay out that dress pattern you rearrange it several times, but it still doesn't fit. Do you toss out the whole works? Of course not. You make short sleeves instead of long, or substitute a border for the hem, or use a contrasting fabric for the pockets, or you just make a blouse instead. These are "creative alternatives."

When you are convinced you can't rearrange your schedule to accommodate an objective, look for other options that will achieve a similar result.

One Christmas I didn't allow enough time to send greeting cards, but at the last minute I defied my schedule and did it anyway. The following year (I hate to admit) the same thing happened. Though I foolishly repeated a planning faux pas, I did learn something from the previous nerve-wracking experience. This time I didn't give in to the pressure, but I still wanted to communicate with my friends. So I dared to break tradition, and designed a New Year's card instead. During the holidays I leisurely addressed envelopes and wrote personal notes. On January 1, I happily, and unharriedly, took a large stack of cards to the post office.

During another planning period, I repeatedly put off inviting two senior citizen friends to dinner because my work load was particularly demanding. It became apparent that it might be another month before I could leisurely have them over. So one evening, as I did miscellaneous tasks around the house, I baked a quiche and homemade muffins. The next day I took portions of both to my friends' homes, along with a little note telling how to warm them for supper. They were surprised and delighted; and one still talks about it—years later—as though it were more special to her than eating a regular meal at my home.

Sharing personal examples like this has its risks, especially if your zany friends are in the audience. When I related this creative alternative at a seminar, a familiar voice murmured from the back of the room, "You never brought *me* quiche and muffins!"

3. Reexamine your objectives. Ask, "Is it worth it?"

A number of years ago I gave a short time-management course to the colleagues I worked with. When we discussed priorities, I encouraged them not to be concerned about low ones. If they are important enough, I said, they will eventually work their way up to number one. Then I mentioned my photo albums, which were ten years behind. Every time I planned, I listed them with my objectives, and they inevitably got a *C* priority.

The wives of two of my colleagues were at our meeting, and nodded knowingly about neglected photo albums. I half-humorously told them, "You'll know planning works when my photo albums are up-to-date."

But a year passed and I didn't get to them. Finally I asked that vital question, "Is it worth it?" Yes, it was, I decided. This was an *important* desire that needed to become *immediate*. I realized that this was an *A* priority that I had treated as a *C* priority. So I cleared my Fourth-of-July weekend to do it. I had already planned to house sit for friends in the mountains, so I took my boxes of albums and unsorted pictures with me. A girl friend came along and brought one of her projects.

I finished the albums and lined them up in a living room bookcase. Countless times over the next couple of weeks I briefly sat on the sofa and admired them whenever I passed through the room—like a kid who sleeps with his new cowboy boots. Then I sent postcards to my two friends and simply said, "Planning works: My photo albums are done!"

Around the same time another goal was consistently getting upstaged—to make candles. I had a folder in my hobby file on candle making, not to mention a huge box of paraffin that was given to me, and (believe it or not) accompanied me on two cross-country moves. I kept telling myself that it was my economical, enterprising responsibility to make candles for gifts. When I asked, "Is it worth it?" my immediate response of relief was, "No." So I gave away the paraffin and file folder and forgot about it.

Suppose you determine an objective is worth accomplishing, but you can't free a weekend—or even an hour—for it? Then you may have to . . .

4. Relinquish what you just can't do. Ask, "What is the worst that can happen if I don't do this?"

Remember the time you shopped frantically for a dress you *had* to have for a social event, even though you had ten more important things to do? Then after several hours of futile searching, you went home empty-handed and ended up wearing something you already had? Two weeks later it probably didn't make a bit of difference in your life.

The fear of what might happen if you abandon an objective is usually far worse than the actual consequence of letting it go. Face the possibilities head on so you don't fret yourself into an ulcer later.

For some months my houseplants needed repotting. But compared to other commitments, they had a low priority. Since I was to be out-of-town for six weeks, I felt forced to squeeze them in and stressed because I couldn't. Finally I asked, "What's the worst that can happen if I don't repot my plants?" The worst, I decided, was that they would all die and I would have to buy new ones. When I actually said it, it didn't sound so bad. In fact, it became easier to live with that likelihood than to worry needlessly. And it put my plants in proper perspective. How often do we sacrifice physical or emotional health over something far too insignificant? As it turned out, an engagement was canceled before I left town, so I tended the plants after all. Ironically, a friend who kept them for me while I was away overwatered them, and they all succumbed to root rot!

If you have a do-or-die mentality toward a task, think of what would happen if you *did* die. It wouldn't get done then either, at least not by you. Remember that you are neither indispensable nor invincible. Don't do the thing that will do you in. Do-or-die may mean do-*and*-die. Learn to use the release valve of relinquishment.

Learn to Troubleshoot

We have just looked at how you can resolve isolated planning problems. But suppose your overall planning track record poses one big problem? You rearrange, replan, reexamine, and relinquish more than you carry out. If that is true for you, reread chapter 10 and look for these possible explanations for your trouble:

1. Unrealistic expectations
    Planning too much
    Planning too closely
    Not planning piecemeal—
        i.e, trying to eat elephants whole
    Not allowing for the unexpected
2. Tyranny of the urgent
    Giving in to distractions
        and unimportant interruptions
    Losing sight of your priorities
3. Jumping process
    Taking planning shortcuts
    Trying to get by
        with fewer planning steps

Summary of Planning Principles

The art of planning is just that—an art. It's a skill you refine and perfect with practice. You learn that some things work for you and some don't. You remain open to new ideas but not under obligation to any of them. You can be as simple or sophisticated a time manager as suits you, as long as you are effective.

I said in the introduction I would give you just the basics; but I encourage you to explore beyond. Browse through books and periodicals that pinpoint specific management issues you are dealing with. Pick up suggestions from your friends and colleagues. Become an eclectic manager—no single source tells it all.

The following summary highlights principles to draw on and pursue further, several of which we have already discussed. Make a notation next to the one(s) you want to work on. These mainly have to do with management techniques. Chapter 17 gives guidelines for using organizational tools.

Personal Planning Pointers

A. The longer the planning period, the less detailed the planning.
B. Plan the predictable; leave ample time for the unpredictable.
C. Work smarter, not harder.
   1. Do difficult tasks when at your best.
   2. Do small jobs regularly to avoid bigger, more time-consuming jobs later.
   3. Delegate whenever you can.
D. Think ahead.
   1. Schedule regular maintenance projects and renewals on your calendar.
   2. Do big projects piecemeal and avoid coming up short in the end.
   3. Don't wait until deadlines. Few things have to be done at the last minute.
   4. Anticipate needs for upcoming projects. Lack of foresight results in wasted time and resources.
   5. Avoid rush hours when you can. When you can't, allow enough time to compensate.
   6. Avoid impulsive errand running. Set a time to do several together.
   7. Take time every night to prepare for the next day.
E. Don't trust your memory.
   1. Write it down (priorities, plans, appointments, etc.).
   2. Check your calendar—and your priorities—before making a commitment.
F. Conserve and control time.
   1. Set deadlines.
   2. Handle papers and correspondence *once*.
   3. Deal with distractions and interruptions—don't drift from priorities.
   4. Develop conversation closures.
   5. Tame the telephone—it should be a time-saver, not a time-killer.
   6. Avoid people who waste time.

7. Determine objectives for meetings and appointments and work toward them.
8. Keep a personal time log—Find out how you use your time versus how you *think* you use it.

G. Plan often-wasted time periods.
　1. Waiting periods—keep projects handy.
　2. Travel time—use it.
　3. Evenings and weekends—make them count.

H. Strike a balance.
　1. Establish a reasonable routine, but not a rigid rut.
　2. Pace yourself; don't push.
　3. Be flexible, but not undisciplined.
　4. Be spontaneous, but not unscheduled.

I. Mind these additional *P*s
　1. Procrastination—"the thief of time"
　　Do something now!
　2. Perfectionism—another time robber
　　Recognize the point of diminishing returns.
　3. Poor punctuality—the thief of *others'* time
　　"If you're five minutes early, you'll
　　never be late!"

J. Give yourself a break.
　1. Learn to live with loose ends.
　2. Reward yourself for completed tasks.
　3. Relax and enjoy life.

14

How to Enjoy
Holidays and Hospitality
Through Planning

Whenever I teach seminars and talk about planning, the subject of holiday hassle inevitably comes up. I'd like to discuss it here to show how a little planning can greatly enhance your enjoyment of the Christmas season.

Is Christmas a crisis at your house? December 25 has a way of creeping up, then suddenly catapulting us into chaos. That we have come to expect the happy holidays to be hectic ones is a sad commentary on our culture. Every year December magazine covers feature articles sure to perpetuate the panic:

"The Holiday Season: Hang in There"
"Make Your Holiday Happier"
"Coping with Holiday Hassles"
"Taking the Stress Out of Shopping"
"Hair-do's in a Hurry"
"Gifts to Buy at the Eleventh Hour"

Little wonder that Scrooge traded peace and good cheer for the bah humbugs. So do many of us.

The Christmas season should be a warm and wonderful time

with family and friends. And it *can* be—if you plan it that way.

When I lived in New York City in my mid-twenties, a friend told me one December day that she never set foot inside a store after Thanksgiving other than to buy groceries. As we crunched down new snow and walked past brightly decorated windows on Fifth Avenue, I said, "Don't you buy gifts?" She replied, "Of course, but I finish my shopping before the mad rush because otherwise it spoils my spirit. If I don't have it by Thanksgiving, I don't get it."

Before that conversation, it never occurred to me to prepare for the holidays before they came. I shopped until the stores closed Christmas Eve and wrapped the last of my presents minutes before we opened them. But I was ready to reform. After years of letting December do me in, I called a truce and have since been cultivating ways to enjoy the season rather than endure it.

If you are ready to raise the white flag on frantic festivities, read on. If you already avoid Christmas chaos, hats off to you. You can skip the rest of this discussion.

Have you ever considered that Christmas involves nearly 10 percent of your year? For most of us, celebrations begin at Thanksgiving and culminate on New Year's Day. Planning can't start too soon. In fact, you are wise to begin in January. "January!" you gasp. "I still have a 'holiday hangover.'" Maybe so, but do you want the holiday heebie-jeebies twelve months later? If you were to reread the first two chapters on planning and apply each principle to Christmas, you would grab your calendar and start to list objectives and priorities in anticipation of the peaceful payoff on December 25.

What *are* your objectives for Christmastime? Last year a friend wrote on her card, "December has been dedicated to fun, family, and festivities. We're having a ball—baking, wrapping, concerting, and Nutcrackering." She's not only a wife and mother of two active sons, but during the fall she taught school and did graduate study as well. Her time for "fun, family, and festivities" didn't come by accident; she *planned* it.

Everyone will have different holiday objectives, but some activities are common to most of us. Let's get those under control so we can concentrate on the spirit of the season.

Greeting Cards. Most stores display their order books in the fall, giving you plenty of lead time. Address a few envelopes every day in October and November and your schedule won't even feel it. If you go the photo route, why not take a fun family shot during your summer vacation? The kids won't change much, and you won't have to round up everyone for a sitting later.

You may choose to create your own cards, and ought to keep a Christmas file with ideas and artwork to draw from. Design it by fall and take it to the printer before Thanksgiving. Some printers offer free red and green ink in December. If your budget is tight and you hold out for the bargain, you can still go ahead and address your envelopes earlier.

When I directed a women's movement, I sent a few hundred valentines every year. I designed the card by December so I could take advantage of the red-ink special (and because February 14 comes close on the tails of New Year's). A friend once saw me bring my cards to the office from the printer, shook her head in chagrin, and moaned, "You have valentines, and I don't even have Christmas cards yet." I knew how she felt. Another friend usually has half of her beautiful homemade gifts finished in November—for the following year! By comparison I always feel behind regardless of how well prepared I am.

Presents.   Unlike my New York friend, I go into stores during December—not to buy, but to browse. I enjoy the decorations and displays when I'm not under pressure to purchase. Okay, I'll admit it: Sometimes I smugly smile at the crazy crowds who are reaping the consequences of procrastination. I always see myself in that crowd—years past—and hope I don't let it happen again.

Stores are just as eager to take your money in February or April or July as they are in December. And you will spend it more wisely when you aren't fighting hundreds of people and rushing to get back home. Remember, too, that media hype at holiday time will pressure you to buy more than you want or can afford.

Whether you buy your gifts or make them with loving hands, spread the effort throughout the year. Get a head start during the after-Christmas sales. When you make a gift, give yourself a reasonable deadline and stick to it. If time runs out, don't redouble your efforts and run yourself down to finish it. Put it aside for the next year and buy a creative alternative. If you give baked goods, candies, or other homemade goodies, be sure to allow plenty of time on your schedule to be in the kitchen. Make your shopping list well in advance, and include the kind of containers or wrapping you need for your delectables. There's no excuse for seeking baskets or apothecary jars at the last minute.

Keep extra little gifts on hand for unexpected callers and for friends you may have overlooked in your planning. Something simple like candles, miniature bread loaves, a holiday hand towel, and so forth.

Don't wait for the post office to announce deadline dates to mail packages. Once the countdown begins, the lines are already out the door. The same goes for Christmas stamps—buy early.

As you gather gifts during the year, keep an inventory of what you have and whom it's for. Use a code if you must divert snoopers. Keep all your receipts in one place for quick access in case a return is necessary. I maintain a general receipt file for clothes, household items, and so forth, and add an envelope marked "Christmas" to consolidate those sales receipts.

Become a sleuth and listen for clues people drop during the year. Note their hobbies, collections, color preferences, sizes, and so on that you can draw on for gift ideas.

One last thought on gifts: Forget trying to be Saint Santa who gives the perfect present every time. Actually, some of the more frivolous items I've received or bestowed seem often to be the favorites. Don't spoil the fun of shopping and sharing by taking it too seriously. Once in a while stop and think, "What's this season all about anyway?"

Decorations.   "Lights, tinsel . . . action!"

The holidays are here, and boxes come out of the garage or attic. As you untangle your strings of lights, you wonder what frame of mind you were in last January when you stuffed them into storage. Tired, that's what. When it's time to dismantle the trimmings, you have had it and don't want to see another ornament or pine needle for a long time. So you put it all out of sight as quickly as you put it out of mind. When Christmas is finished, you are finished with Christmas, right?

As exciting as it is to put up decorations, it is anticlimactic to take them down. But consider it part of the package, and give it your best for the sake of next year. Pack up everything systematically and inventory your supplies. Number each box, list the contents, and keep the information in a handy place. This takes little extra time and facilitates decorating each year. Write down what you are short on, or what you want to replace. Then you will know exactly what to buy as soon as new merchandise is out next season. Better yet, get what you can at this year's sales. Either way, you avoid having to halt or hold off tree trimming to run out for ornament hangers or a new string of lights.

It's fun to make your own decorations when you can do it at a leisurely pace. If crafts or needlework in December ads and displays inspire you, but your schedule is already full, buy the materials when they're reduced and make them for the following year. I saved 50 percent on a table runner and placemats to cross-stitch and enjoyed working on them now and then during the year. Most onlookers queried Christmas trees in July, but on second thought they commented, "Hmmm, you're smart to start now."

Work with a theme for easier decorating. And work at it together, if you're a family. This part of Christmas contributes to good fellowship and fond memories.

However you deck the halls—elaborately or simply—dedicate your home to a happy holiday spirit.

P.S. Don't wait until the last minute to decorate *yourself.* Line up what you will wear to festive events and book hair appointments early.

Eating and Feasting.   Menu planning is a big timesaver. I recommend it year round, but particularly at this busy time, and especially if you host out-of-town guests, because you want to be free to spend time with them.

If you have a freezer, prepare as much as you can ahead. Plan simple, nutritious meals, and try to avoid fast foods and TV dinners. If ever you need three square meals a day, this is the time. Please allow me to briefly digress on this soapbox.

Doctors' offices are filled in January with Christmas casualties. Colds and flu find easy targets in bodies loaded with sugar and depleted of nutrients. I don't suggest you give up yuletide yummies and carry your own carrots to an open house. But don't give up what's good for you either. You will suffer as much or more from what you don't eat as from what you do.

People tend to miss meals at this time of year because they are on the run and simply don't bother to eat; or they purposely skip a meal so they can indulge at a party. But you need good nutrition to offset the extra sweets and starches you'll consume. Also, whole foods satisfy you, so you are less apt to fill up on snacks mainly made of empty calories.

Even your treats can be good for you. One of my favorite Christmas traditions is munching on fresh-roasted nuts. After Thanksgiving the nutcracker came out and my dad shelled everything from filberts to almonds. Mom roasted them, and my brothers and I consumed them. Two snacks I like to make now are honey-nut corn and dried fruit balls rolled in unsweetened coconut or chopped nutmeats. Your guests will probably appreciate nutritious goodies. Many people today are avoiding empty calories and leaning toward healthier foods.

Don't deprive yourself of delectables—they're half the fun of the season. But be sensible. I've seen people work hard all year on their diet and lose control during the holidays. Then they struggle to get back to good eating habits later. It's not worth it. End of soapbox!

Entertaining—Holiday and Everyday

There's no place like home for the holidays . . . unless home is a havoc. The hectic holidays are often synonymous with the harried hostess. With so much to do, tempers are sometimes as short as time. For every person who tells me of warm family Christmases, another remembers yearly tension and strife—and mother usually takes the rap.

However unfair it may seem, the woman in the home is the one who sets the tone and creates the atmosphere. Many a mom pulls off the season's best party, but leaves her family in the wake of her whirlwind. Frantic entertaining is never worth the expense of other members of the household. Plan only what you can comfortably carry out. This is no time to keep up with the Joneses—or yourself, for that matter.

I love to give a holiday brunch, and intended to start a yearly tradition. One November I finalized my December schedule, and realized I was too tired to host a big affair. I preferred a quiet, uneventful Christmas, yet still wanted to share the season with friends. So instead of one demanding, gala event, I set aside a week of before-dinner hours and invited two or three people to drop over each evening for hors d'oeuvres and wassail (my special brew of fresh, hot fruit juices). The fellowship was some of the richest and most relaxed I've had, and it didn't require a major commitment from any of us. In fact, my friends enjoyed the break en route from work to their home or the shopping center, and were probably glad not to have another fancy function to go to.

Plan Ahead.   My point is, entertaining—holiday or otherwise—doesn't have to be elegant to be enjoyable. Nor should working limit you. It just means you do that much more in advance. If you are having guests after a day at the office, you can set the table the night before and lay out all your serving dishes so you don't search for them when you put the meal on. You can start to make ice cubes several days ahead and line up candles and clean linens for your table. The list goes on, but you get the idea. Don't save anything for the last minute that you can get ready early. Did you ever think to wash vegetables and brew tea for iced drinks the day before a dinner party?

Keep Records.   If you entertain often, work out of a special notebook for party planning. Keep records of who came and what you served. Immediately after the event, write comments for future reference, such as dishes that were a hit, food combinations that worked well, ingredients or amounts you would change next time, and so on.

On each menu-planning page, include every item you will serve, the location of the recipe, the number of recipes to make (one, half, double), the specific ingredients to gather, and a preparation timetable. Before you shop for the occasion, go over the entire list and check off what you already have. Cover everything—don't assume a spice or staple is in your cupboard.

Be Flexible.   Try different kinds of entertaining. And keep in mind that too much planning will spoil an informal affair, while too little will spoil a formal one. When I decided to part with perfectionism, I began to have more casual get-togethers and spontaneous socials in my home. But I still enjoy doing a gourmet dinner, and I plan it down to the toothpicks so I can relax when I put it on. If you know everything is under control, you will be too. But it's hard to be a gracious hostess when you are uptight. Inadequate planning for a formal affair creates anxiety and the event comes off poorly.

Do What You Do Best.   *Vogue* magazine published a lengthy article in which thirteen of this country's most celebrated hosts and hostesses shared their personal secrets. As I began to read it, I thought, "Now I will know how to put on the perfect party." One person said it was in the table settings, another swore by a strategic seating of guests, while others credited the flowers, the hired musicians, and the exotic dessert. By the time I read the last interview, I knew what it takes to be the hostess with the mostess: doing what *you* do best and enjoying it.

Enjoy Your Friends.   Amy Vanderbilt expressed some thoughts about entertaining that fit in so well with my own beliefs about the importance of opening your home to your friends:

Entertaining is like any other skill, the more you practice it the better you become. . . . The good hostess gives the kind of party she can manage well, in which she is most comfortable, that is within her own limitations, the limitations of her household and her house. One woman I know, while her children were in their destructive teens, had no redecoration of any kind done in her house. The parties she gave were all informal and in spring and summer out of doors. It wasn't until her children got into college that she gave the pleasantly formal small dinner parties for which she became noted.

To entertain is to communicate with one's friends. The need for such breaking of bread goes back to primitive times. For us to turn our backs on anything so basic as this human need because of all the real and imagined pressures of our society is destructive. No matter what your economic or even physical situation may be, you can still give parties and you should. . . . A home in which no entertainment takes place is a shell. The owners are only half-functioning.[1]

If you don't already make a point of having friends over, consider incorporating it into your social or home goals. The fellowship is bound to add to the quality of life that makes your house a home.

PART FOUR

How Do You Put It All Together?

Our life is frittered away by detail. . . . Simplify, simplify.
HENRY DAVID THOREAU

15

Discipline:
Doing What Doesn't
Come Naturally

On November 24, 1982, a twenty-five-year-old woman finished the New York Marathon. Big deal, you say? It isn't—until you learn that she had cerebral palsy and was the first woman to ever complete a marathon on crutches.

Linda Down crossed the finish line at 9:40 P.M., eleven hours after she started, and long after the streets were cleared of all the other runners. During the twenty-six-mile race she fell more than a dozen times, once into a pile of glass; but she got right up and kept on going. A reporter remarked that her handicap limited her speed but not her determination. Linda said she did it because she wanted to see if she could make it.

Writing on the importance of willpower, A. Victor Segno observes, "A great many people possess strong Wills, but the majority do not . . . . This fact accounts for some people being successful and famous, while others are not known outside of their neighborhood . . . . A strong Will never hesitates or falters after a decision has been made. It steadily perseveres until the purpose is accomplished . . . . The Will may seem to be strong, because one is able to throw enormous energy into some special effort, but this is no criterion. Its strength is tested by the ability to carry [it] out."[1] Henry Wadsworth Longfellow said, "Great is the art of beginning, but greater the art is of ending." Goals and plans do you no good if you don't carry them out. How nice it would be if we all had a resident genie who made every wish a command, every ambition a fait accompli. But between each intent and accomplishment is a dynamic called discipline.

Why is discipline a mark of the minority? I don't know. But I suspect it has something to do with the fact that everyone wants the prize, but few will pay the price. Further, most of us do not even consider the cost to begin with.

Following one of Paderewski's great performances, a patron of the arts impulsively said to him, "I'd give my life to play like that." The brilliant pianist replied, "I did."

Talent and accomplishment often belie effort. They are deceptive because when we see the product, we don't see the pain and perseverance that produced it. So we credit the achiever with brains, brawn, or lucky breaks and let ourselves off the hook because we fall short in all three.

Not that we could all be concert pianists if we exercised enough discipline. Rather, each of us has the makings of success in some endeavor, but we will only realize it to the extent that we apply our wills to working at it.

William James said, "Anything the mind can believe and conceive, it can achieve." When you determine goals and objectives for your life, you should *expect* to accomplish them and not stop until you do. I have a strong hunch that our failure to turn desires into deeds results more from wafting wills than legitimate limitations. How often do we shelve our well-laid plans without a fight when they meet with resistance? Rather, we would be wise to heed the opening lines of Dr. Scott Peck's fine work *The Road Less Traveled:* "Life is difficult. This is a great truth ... because once we truly see this truth, we transcend it. Once we truly know that life is difficult ... then life is no longer difficult. Because once it is accepted, the fact that life is difficult no longer matters."[2] Discipline meets with the difficulties and makes a way through.

How, then, can we acquire this quality of stick-to-itiveness? I don't know that either. I have often hoped for an antidote to cure my own vacillating volition. A simple solution. A fast formula. For me, as I emphasized early on, help in these matters concerning time management comes more in a mind-set than in a method. This chapter deals with a particular mind-set that has rescued my waning will more than once and may come to your aid too. I don't think discipline will ever be easy. But I do think a better understanding can make it more desirable, thus more eagerly exercised.

Won't Power

The ancient Chinese philosopher Mencius said, "Men must be decided on what they will not do, and then they are able to act with vigor in what they ought to do." Four centuries later Jesus taught, "Let your yes be yes, and your no, no."

Discipline means choices. Your plans and priorities reflect the choices you make. But what they don't show are all the options you *don't* choose. Every time you say yes to a goal or objective, you say no to many more. It is important that you give as much thought to the nos as to the yeses. In other words, *won't power* is as necessary as willpower. Every prize has its price. The prize is the yes; the price is the no. Before you embark on a pursuit, take into account what is required of you.

A suddenly widowed mother of three told of her decision to invest her insurance settlement in an education. She carefully considered what four years of studying would mean and faced the reality of a tight budget and precious little time for diversion. But it seemed a small price to pay in light of the doors her degree would open and the increased earning ability she could expect. Her children supported her decision, knowing that a little hardship now would be more than made up for later. Today she is a financial consultant with a lucrative income.

I continue to quote Dr. Peck, without apology, because his insights are so helpful to this discussion. He says that one of the tools of discipline is "delaying gratification." "Delaying gratification is a process of scheduling the pain and pleasure of life in such a way as to enhance the pleasure by meeting and experiencing the pain first and getting it over with. It is the only decent way to live."[3]

Delaying gratification is, basically, exercising won't power. It pertains to daily decisions as well as longer-term resolves. You delayed gratification as a youngster if you ate your vegetables first, so you could enjoy the rest of your dinner. You delay gratification now when you clean house instead of window shopping, so you can go to the beach on the weekend; when you forego a beautiful pair of shoes because you are saving for a coat; or when you go to bed instead of staying up for the movie because you have an important day ahead and need your sleep.

It helps to use "rewards" as incentives to finish a task or a major part of a task. Some would say discipline is its own reward, that the end goal is motivation enough. I suppose it should be, but I am not so noble. Looking forward to breaks helps me maintain momentum. Most of us need interludes in our work to take a walk, sip a cup of tea, eat a snack, watch our favorite program, take a catnap—whatever revives and refreshes us. Your breathers don't need to be extended, just enough to shake out the cobwebs and give some relief.

Never confuse willpower and won't power with rigidity. Discipline doesn't mean you serve a set of standards without ever veering from them. It means you try to make choices consistent with your purpose and priorities, *and* your general well-being at any given time. So on one cleaning day you may need to be tough on yourself and finish the housework even though you don't feel like doing it, while another cleaning day you may need to leave the vacuum cleaner in the closet and read a book. This spirit of flexibility also allows you to drop everything for a friend in need, but does not oblige you to indulge every phone interruption during the course of a day.

Sometimes choosing *not* to comply with your predetermined course of action is the best choice at the time, because it serves your purposes more in the long run. A verbal whip that women commonly wield to their detriment is the "I blew it" lash. Every time you say that, you kill discipline, because eventually you'll figure that since you can't be perfect, you might as well not try at all.

Perfection is not the reason to be disciplined. Rather, discipline should result in peace of mind because you are in charge of yourself. Being in charge means knowing what you need most, and meeting that need when you can. One afternoon you may need the satisfaction of completing an undesirable task; another, you may need the grace to back off and relax. Sometimes eating that hot fudge sundae just may not be such a bad choice. So instead of saying, "I blew it," try this: "I generally stay away from desserts, but today I'm going to enjoy a big one!"

I heard a wise mother say, "I will keep sugar and white flour from my children only until doing so hurts their psyches more than it helps their health." The principle applies across the board. Before you bullheadedly browbeat yourself to carry out your intentions, or mercilessly malign yourself when you don't, consider that you may have needed to change gears just to feel intact. Likewise, don't let anyone put you on a guilt trip when you stick to your schedule instead of giving in to everyone's interruptive whims.

Discipline for discipline's sake is nothing more than chronic compulsion and drives one to rigid performance and unrelenting perfectionism. True discipline achieves a balance of producing, but not pushing; of diligence, not driving. Dr. Peck explains that "balancing is the discipline that gives us flexibility. . . . To be organized and efficient, to live wisely, we must daily delay gratification and keep an eye on the future, yet to live joyously we must also possess the capacity, when it is not destructive, to live in the present and act spontaneously. In other words, discipline itself must be disciplined."[4]

Discipline is the mark of maturity. It is "the ability to regulate conduct by principle and judgment rather than by impulse, desire, high pressure, or social custom. It is basically the ability to *subordinate*."[5] The Bible says that it is better to have self-control than to control an army. Discipline separates the women from the girls and makes way for success, achievement, and fulfillment. It has well been said that the world belongs to the disciplined.

If your attempts to subordinate your will keep running into brick walls, ask "why" before you berate yourself because you've failed. An overweight woman came to me during a seminar and said, "I'm so undisciplined. I can't stick to a diet and my house is always a mess. I feel like a slob." It wasn't too hard to detect her accusing voice. So I observed, "You're not totally undisciplined. You made it to this conference, you arrive promptly to each session, and you are neatly dressed." She almost smiled, and then I added, "There's probably a *reason* why you haven't been able to lose weight or get your home in order." She looked as though I had given her a reprieve from death row and said, "Really?"

Later I found out there was a very big reason. She was widowed just a year before. Her husband was an alcoholic who verbally abused her all twenty-four years of their marriage. It never occurred to her that her poor self-image was keeping her from effecting positive changes in her life. It was the first time I saw someone become happy over discovering low self-esteem. In the realization, she saw hope. She decided to get counseling and to affirm herself before attacking her weight problem. Meanwhile, some of her friends offered to go to her house and help her clean it up to boost her morale.

Right Thinking

Oliver Wendell Holmes said, "The rule of joy and the law of duty seem to me all one." Discipline means you get past the drudgery and see the delight. Not that everything you do will become enjoyable, but that the end result is desirable.

A woman at one of my seminars told me that her six-year-old daughter swam with a team and practiced every morning for an hour, during which she did two thousand to three thousand meters. She related a brief conversation her daughter had with a family friend:

"Do you like swimming?"

"Yes, I love it."

"Is it fun?"

"No!"

That six-year-old learned what many sixty-year-olds never experience: the joy of discipline.

Computer operators use a term that applies here: GIGO— garbage in, garbage out. If you program yourself with negative thoughts about your tasks, you can't expect much in the way of positive results. "Our mental attitude in the use of time is most important. If we don't want to do something, we can find a thousand reasons for not doing it. . . . But if we want to do something nothing will stop us—obstacles are brushed aside as if they were nothing."[6]

The key to right thinking about discipline is *wanting* to do something. Unfortunately the very word *discipline* puts us off because it sounds restrictive and punitive. We must squelch the nasty notion that treats it as a truant officer, stalking us to make sure we tow the line: "Use every minute"; "Don't goof off"; "Eat this"; "Don't eat that"; and on and on. That's not discipline, that's the "inner critic" we talked about in chapter 2, who's out to make your life miserable and keep you ineffective. True discipline isn't on your back needling you with imperatives; true discipline is on your side, nudging you with incentives. When you can understand that discipline is self-caring, not self-castigating, you won't cringe at its mention, but will cultivate it for your benefit.

The best way to start thinking rightly is to clean up your vocabulary. Get rid of these words: *should, should have; shouldn't, shouldn't have; ought, ought not; must, must not; have to, got to, need to.* They drain the desire out of discipline and the life out of you.

Occasionally I catch myself thinking, *I have to exercise,* or *I shouldn't eat that,* rather than *I want to exercise,* and *I don't want to eat that.* You may say, "It's just a matter of semantics. What difference does it make?" Actually, it makes a lot of difference.

Dr. John Diamond, president of the International Academy of Preventive Medicine, wrote a book that gives evidence of how such thoughts literally strengthen or weaken our bodies. In the middle of our chest, just beneath the upper part of the breastbone, is the thymus gland. Though little was known of its purpose or function before the 1950s, we now have evidence that it contributes to muscular contraction and helps to maintain an effective immune system. Dr. Diamond writes that "the thymus gland is the first organ to be affected ... by an emotional state" and explains that a pleasant thought strengthens it, while an unpleasant thought weakens it. "Unfortunately," he says, "95 percent of the people I have tested have an underactive thymus gland. This means that most of us are involved too much with unpleasantnesses."[7]

Medicine and psychology agree that positive thoughts promote health, while negative thoughts may foster disease. We are stressed enough by the discord all around us, without having to create our own. Since discipline is so daily, it can become a powerhouse of fulfillment if you turn it into a positive force.

This is not the Pollyanna positive thinking I warned against early in the book. This is that *proper* thinking toward productive ends. It is not lying to yourself and saying you want to do something you really don't (Your thymus knows the difference!). It is seeing the good in the difficult and wanting it despite the discomfort.

Many a person's downfall in discipline comes in trying to change a bad habit. They often fail because they focus on the undesirable behavior. If you want to change something, concentrate on a new behavior to take its place.

To illustrate my point, consider eating habits. Countless people tell me they would like to eat better, but they don't want to "give up" tasty food. They equate nutrition with dull cuisine and deprivation. Women say, "My family will never go without that." I always ask them if they replace what they remove with something just as enjoyable, and their typical response is that they never thought about it. So I suggest that instead of thinking of what they *can't* have, they think about what they *can* eat. Fruit juice with sparkling mineral water is a delicious substitute for soft drinks; and snacks and cookies prepared with whole grains and dried fruits give candy bars good competition. It isn't easy to change old habits, because they burrow their way into our lives. But you can always reroute the river! Right thinking helps you navigate a new course.

Writing on *The Disciplined Life,* author Richard Taylor noted a "shift of interest from the intellectual to the recreational." He cited the change in the last couple of decades from the popularity of intercollegiate debates to the more popularly attended sports events. Obviously, he acknowledged, some discipline is required for athletic training. "But the discipline of the mind is on a higher level." He observed that both a disciplined body and a disciplined mind "are but adjuncts of a disciplined character. This is the great lack, the fatal deficiency. Too many of us are weak as persons."[8]

It is the person, not a prescription, that brings about right thinking. Invariably after I speak at length about discipline, someone will ask impatiently, "But how do you make it work?" I think I've finally figured out what that person is asking: "How can I have my cake and eat it too?" You can't.

Igor Gorin, the famous Ukrainian-American baritone, told of his early days studying voice. He loved to smoke a pipe, but one day his professor told him, "Igor, you will have to make up your mind whether you are going to be a great singer, or a great pipe smoker. You cannot be both." So the pipe went.

Discipline works; it's people who malfunction. When the spirit is willing, but the flesh is weak, what discipline boils down to is . . .

Mind Over Matter

Syndicated radio commentator Mort Crim aired the following editorial:

> It's become almost a ritual around our house to ask our son at bedtime, or when he comes in from play, "Well, did you have fun today?"
> It's almost as though having fun has become the new success standard. If an activity is fun, then it must be worthwhile.

And maybe we're communicating a false sense of value to our children. The fact is, many worthwhile endeavors aren't fun; and where did we ever get the idea anyway that life was SUPPOSED to be just one long-running game? True, all work and no play makes Johnny a dull boy. But on the other hand, trying to turn everything we do into play makes for terrible frustrations. Because life—even the most rewarding life—includes activities and circumstances which aren't fun at all.

I like my job as a journalist—it's satisfying, it's personally rewarding, it's often pleasurable, but believe me, it *isn't* ALWAYS fun. Psychoanalyst Erika Freeman says we're suffering from fun-pollution. Well, its an established fact that disciplined people are happier people. So maybe we ought to go back to grandmother's approach: She never used to say, eat your vegetables because it'll be fun. Grandmother would tell it like it was: You eat those vegetables because they're good for you.[9]

We're a society of softies. The prevailing philosophy goes, "If it feels good, do it; if it doesn't, don't." Take mornings, for instance. Who wants to leave a comfortable, cozy bed to face another day? But we have to eventually, so delaying it seems to me unnecessary punishment. I came to that conclusion after years of morning misery.

I remember school days and Mom's regular reveille: "Time to get up!" I agonized in bed until the eleventh hour and ran my mother's patience short because she had to repeat her call many times. Then I went away to college and had to get myself up. I was tired of waging war with waking, and I also observed the potential efficacy of the early hours. Since most of the girls slept in, it seemed an advantageous time to study. For several days I gave myself pep talks about why I should rise and shine early. They didn't help. Finally I decided that when the alarm rang, I would rise—just because I wanted to, and regardless of how I felt. It worked, and has worked ever since. Not that I don't enjoy an occasional lazy morning under the covers, but usually I get up early without the aid of clocks or calls.

I don't for one moment wish to imply that everyone should be an early bird. Your biorhythms just may not cooperate as mine do. But the point is, whatever is important to you is within your resources to accomplish; and it may take a few swift kicks!

Dr. David Burns says that "Motivation does not come first, *action* does! You have to prime the pump." To reverse the order is to put the cart before the horse. "You foolishly wait until you feel in the mood to do something. Since you don't feel like doing it, you automatically put it off." Rather, he explains, it's often *after* we get involved in a task that we become highly motivated. "When someone suggests you do something, you whine, 'I don't *feel* like it.' Well, who said you were supposed to feel like it? If you wait until you're 'in the mood,' you may wait forever!"[10]

Sometimes willpower means that push must come to shove. When the water in the pool is goose-bump cold, you're smarter to just jump in than to prolong the discomfort by wading slowly.

Theodore Roosevelt warned: "The things that will destroy America are prosperity at any price, peace at any price, safety first instead of duty first, the love of soft living, and the get-rich theory of life."

Perhaps William James offered sound advice when he said, "Do every day or two something for no other reason than that you would rather not do it."

Our Disciplined Best

Discipline is habit-forming. A little leads to more, because the benefits prove increasingly desirable. Unfortunately the opposite is also true: A weak will spirals downward, and establishes a pattern of irresponsibility. Thus, discipline, or lack of, has a domino effect.

You've seen what happens when dominoes are lined up, then toppled by a chain reaction after the first one falls. In the same way, lack of discipline in one area of your life automatically influences the others. For example, when you slough off in the physical dimension—disregarding proper diet, exercise, and rest—you will slowly slacken your commitment to other areas as well. You may produce less in a work day, be more inclined to watch television reruns than to accomplish a goal, eventually become depressed. Neglect in discipline comes on insidiously. Once it sets in, we write off our purposes, plans, and priorities, and take the path of least resistance.

But you will find out, if you haven't already, that indulgence immobilizes. We tend to not realize it until it already controls us, then we have to redouble our willpower to reverse the spiral. At those times you may wonder if it's worth it; but when you finally overcome inertia, you will feel better all around. We are happier, *and* healthier, when at our best; and we are at our best when we are disciplined.

Beware of extended periods of self-pity. We all need a little pampering once in a while. In fact, a psychologist told me that it does us good to feel sorry for ourselves now and then. But prolonged personal pathos will undo discipline. The reverse is true, too. Stepped-up Spartanism can revitalize a discouraged spirit and set you back on course.

Some call discipline the door to liberation. Viktor Frankl learned to be free while imprisoned in Nazi concentration camps. "It is not freedom from conditions," he said, "but freedom to take a stand toward the conditions." He proposed that "the Statue of Liberty on the East Coast be supplemented by a Statue of Responsibility on the West Coast."[11]

Freedom is the right *and* responsibility to choose how we will live. We are free to be disciplined or undisciplined. The question is, when are we freer?

"The cultivation of the Will Power is without doubt the first duty every person owes to himself and to his family. Without a strong Will he can have neither firmness, independence nor individuality of character. Without it he cannot give truth its full force, or morals their proper guidance, nor save himself from being the slave of other people."[12]

Discipline: the door to liberation, and the gateway to life!

16

Managing
Your Space

We are a nation of pack rats. If you have any doubts, count the number of garage sales advertised in your local newspaper this weekend. Probably every one of us, given a few hours notice, could gather up enough discards to post our own sign.

We not only accumulate junk, but we acquire a lot of nice things that we don't need. One of the greatest ironies of this age is that our multitudinous labor-saving gadgets and devices quite often hamper our efficiency instead of help it. We are tyrannized by things and hindered by having.

The burden of ownership has invoked fair warning throughout centuries and nations. The Chinese declared, "To have little is to possess. To have plenty is to be perplexed." French philosopher Voltaire thought that the happiest of mortals was he who is above everything he possesses. Chaucer, the English poet, said "Fie on possession." Spanish writer Santayana vowed, "Private wealth I should decline, or any sort of personal possessions, because they would take away my liberty." And our own Walt Whitman contemplated living with the animals because "they are so placid and self-contain'd. . . . Not one is dissatisfied, not one is demented with the mania of owning things."

Managing your time is a losing battle if you don't manage your space. Letting unnecessary articles collect in your closets and cupboards is like allowing unimportant activites to crowd your calendar. Both have to go. Even the Bible says there's a time to keep and a time to throw away. One writer recommends "pitching the excess baggage." Another suggests we "eliminate and concentrate." Anne Morrow Lindbergh says it well, ". . . the art of shedding: how little one can get along with, not how much."

I call it "clutter cleanup." The dictionary defines clutter as, "a jumble; confusion; disorder." Those are the same effects it has on your life. When your home contains clutter, you unconsciously carry it with you wherever you go. You may think you've closed the door on it, but it fetters you nonetheless.

When friends ask me to help them get their life in order, this is where I begin. Before I ask if they have a purpose or a goal or a plan, I ask, "Do you have clutter?" Then I advise them to get rid of it. They always call me afterward and exclaim, "You were right." Then they tell me how free and unencumbered they feel. Several have added, "I had no idea that stuff affected me so much."

Do *you* have clutter? If you compare yourself to your neighbor who has a garage full of relics, it may seem that you don't. On second thought, however, do any of these remarks sound familiar?

"It may come in handy someday."

"I put a lot of time/energy/money into it."

"I don't want to hurt Aunt Addie's feelings."

"I've kept it this long . . ."

"It may be valuable someday."

"I'll get around to it eventually."

I had to ask myself some hard-nosed questions when I began to clean out my clutter. And I still ask them because clutter has an irritating way of showing up again just when I think I've licked it. If you can't decide what constitutes clutter, but you have some questionable articles, quiz yourself and see what you come up with.

1. Does this serve a function, or does it just take up space?

One woman at a seminar immediately reacted to this. She pictured a stark home with bare essentials and argued, "I *like* having paintings on my walls." "I do, too," I agreed, "because they serve an aesthetic function." I'm talking about the things you dust around every week, that elicit more aggravation than affection—like the broken knickknacks and silly souvenirs; or the things that you once used, or intended to use, but don't— like the rusty exercycle, or the french-fry cutter, or the unidentifiable pottery you received as a wedding gift ten years ago.

I know a woman who has a trunk full of wigs, props, and old clothes. In some homes it would be clutter. But in hers, it's almost essential. A born comedienne, she can be counted on to liven any meeting or party with an original skit. The key is, do you use it?

2. Is this meaningful, or is it misplaced sentiment?

Many a thing kept in the name of nostalgia is just a plain nuisance. Family heirlooms *can* be wonderful treasures, but one person's heirloom can also be another person's headache. Don't keep things for the sake of someone else's memory if it doesn't have a place in your heart or home. I turned down my grandmother's china doll because I knew it would lie in a drawer. But the petite rocking chair she needlepointed for me when I was a little girl will stay with me forever.

3. Does this inspire or depress?

Beware of unfinished projects that churn up more guilt than motivation. For me, it was yards of fabric and piles of patterns. In college and early career years, I made most of my clothes. As my work and life-style changed, so did my interest in sewing. But I hung on to all my supplies, thinking any all-American woman *should* make her own clothes. Occasionally, to appease the guilt, I decided to sew something. Either it didn't turn out, or I didn't finish it. More guilt. One of the most liberating days in my life was when I said, "I don't *want* to sew, and I don't *have* to sew," and gave it all away. I did keep my sewing machine for crafts and mending, but I was prepared to say good-bye to that, too, if it haunted me.

4. Does this contribute to "hobbying" or hoarding?

Collecting is an art; accumulating is an addiction. Long after I stopped teaching school, I kept saving cottage-cheese cartons, strawberry baskets, and tofu trays. "Think of all the cute crafts I could make with them." Of course I never did, and they kept piling up. When I caught on to clutter clutching, I unloaded them on a day-care worker who *could* use them. But I still collect miniature wooden animals because I like them and it's fun.

Making the Break

What do you do with this stuff called clutter? Gather it up and clear it out! Here are four steps to making the break:

1. Decide what should go.

Systematically go through your rooms and storage areas. Some clutter will be obvious—it's been driving you crazy for a long time, but you just haven't done anything about it. Other objects you may hem and haw over. Ask the four questions and answer them truthfully. Sometimes it helps to have a friend or family member give objective input.

Put similar items together—such as clothes, tools, books, and so forth. It's also a good idea to separate still functional articles from those that are unusable or inoperable, since you will send them in different directions.

2. Determine a plan.

A major deterrent to dumping clutter is not knowing what to do with it. Personally, I hesitate to throw out good things, but I more readily relinquish them when I know someone can benefit from their use. If you have a lot to dispose of, consider it a goal and make it a priority. Remember, you won't be as effective overall until it's gone.

Charities are the most obvious and common recipients for your discards—Goodwill, Salvation Army, and others. But there are many other options. For instance, churches may welcome wearable clothing to help needy families in their community or to send to deprived countries where they have missionaries. Halfway houses, battered wives centers, homes for unwed mothers are other places that need supplements for their low budgets. If you give away clothing, make sure the pieces are clean and presentable. Poverty-stricken people are not without pride. Any time you donate things to one of these concerns, ask for a receipt that you can use for a tax deduction.

Garage sales and resale shops offer opportunities to get a little back on your discards. Schools, libraries, and rest homes may want your books and magazines. Some missions take used eyeglasses. Make phone calls and track down organizations you can contribute to.

During my brief time of teaching, I laboriously collected and categorized instruction aids that filled two long files. I was tempted to keep the product of my hard work when I left the profession, because I couldn't bear to dump it. At the same time my church was beginning a private school, and it occurred to me to ask if they might want my material. The librarian was pleased to have it, and I was happy it could be used. Many times since, I have been glad I gave it up then, because it would be outdated now. This points out another good reason for giving up certain items. If you hold onto them too long, they may no longer be of use to anyone.

3. Stick to your guns.

Treat your clutter like a doctor has to treat a disease—unemotionally. Hit it head on, and do what you need to do. You may even have to be ruthless. If sentiment doesn't get to you, your pocketbook might. Once everything is gathered in one spot, dollar signs may start flashing, and you are apt to back off because you just can't throw "money" away. Don't think of clutter that way. In the first place, it isn't as though you redeem the actual value of anything simply by keeping it. Second, and most important, consider what your peace of mind is worth. Because that is what you may be gaining by giving up those articles.

4. Still hanging on?

There's a last resort for people with parting pains. You don't *have* to do anything drastic immediately. Put what you can't part with in bags or boxes, seal and date them, and make a general notation on the outside concerning the contents (clothes, shoes, etc.). If you haven't missed anything in six months to a year, donate it *without* opening it again. If you look inside, you'll justify keeping it all over again.

I'm often asked, "Have you ever tossed something and later regretted getting rid of it?" A few times. But given the choice of taking back with it everything else I threw out, there is no question that I would rather never see it again.

Keeping It Under Control

Clutter is like weeds; it keeps coming back. But once you do an initial purge, it is easier to keep it under control. Parkinson's Law states that work expands to fill the time available. A slight revision applies to this discussion: Clutter expands to fill the space available. Before you bring something new home, ask, "Do I need it?" not "Can I use it?" I have a little agreement with myself about clothes—when I buy a new item, I eliminate an old one. Otherwise, I figure I don't need it.

Beware of people who pass off their clutter to you because they don't have the nerve to dispose of it themselves. I visited a friend who showed me a set of antique linen hand towels and asked if I thought they were pretty. Yes, I said, they *are* lovely. "Good," she said as she handed them to me, "you can have them. I just don't have the room, but they're too pretty to throw away."

I share with a few close friends a tradition that keeps us from collecting clutter. It's called the "memory plan." On red-letter occasions, mainly our birthdays and Christmas, we give each other a good time instead of a gift. We may go to dinner and a

play, or take a weekend trip, or buy our favorite snacks and
have a Scrabble marathon—a special time together we can remember and talk about fondly. Last Christmas a man I know
who is on a tight budget gave all his friends his "time"—to
help them with projects or repairs around the house. Baby-
sitting for a frazzled friend so she can have some time alone
might be the best present you could give her. When we think of
gifts, we too often think only of things. But we can also give
ourselves in meaningful ways.

Cleaning up your clutter does not mean you have to become
a neatness fanatic. When you get rid of things, chances are
you'll get rid of a few messes too. But compulsively keeping
everything in place is not the objective here. Too much attention to neatness can be defeating—like Sisyphus rolling a
heavy stone uphill only to have it roll down again. Neatness
can also be deceptive—if you carefully organize your clutter as
I once did. My shelves and drawers were totally tidy, but full of
things I had no business keeping.

I *have* observed an interesting phenomenon among women
who become effective time managers. Those who once were
quite messy become more orderly; and those who were overly
meticulous begin to tolerate a little disarray. There's a happy
medium for each of us; and we must operate according to our
own design.

According to Your Own Style

Frankly, I've come to appreciate all kinds of housekeepers
and even find intrigue in how they "run their ship." I've stayed
in a lot of homes and observed a variety of domestic engineers.
I can't say one way is best, because it isn't. The end result is
what counts. Harmony, both in operations and in relations,
seems to me the greater goal. I like a home that feels lived in
and "loved in." Whether or not that is accomplished with a few
strewn socks and some dirty dishes is secondary. Whatever
your style, the absence of clutter is sure to help you get back to
basics. The story that follows illustrates so well the point I am
trying to make.

On an early spring day in Washington, D.C., a new excursion boat was making its way up the Potomac on its maiden run. To inaugurate this event, a large number of Congressmen and senators had been invited, along with some members of the press. The sun was bright and hot, and one famous senator had removed his shoes and socks and settled back in a deck chair to wiggle his toes. The socks were hung on a railing in front of him.

One of the columnists aboard was observing all this when someone running along the deck inadvertently brushed against one of the socks. It fell over the railing into the river and was quickly swallowed in the wake of the ship. The columnist was particularly impressed by what followed next, and it confirmed in his mind this legislator's true genius. The senator, seeing what had happened, calmly went over to the railing, picked up his remaining sock and threw it overboard. Writing about the incident later, the columnist confessed that if the same thing had happened to him, he would have taken the one remaining sock and put it in his pocket and brought it home. "I have a whole drawerful of single socks at home. I won't ever find the mate, but one cannot throw away a perfectly good single sock. My life is full of single socks. Things that have no possible use for me. . . . I've got to clean out all the things that are perfectly good, but good for nothing, and get down to some simple basics."[1]*

What are the odd socks in *your* life?

* From *There's a Lot More to Health Than Not Being Sick* by Bruce Larson, copyright © 1980 by Bruce Larson; used by permission of Word Books, Publisher, Waco, Texas.

17

Organizational
Tools and Tips

In the opening lines of *Megatrends*, John Naisbitt said the most explosive transformation taking place today is the megashift from an industrial to an information society. Our war with time is largely a war with information. While it seems we have too much to do, the reality is that we have too much to remember.

Naisbitt holds that information is no longer a resource but an enemy, unless we know what to do with it. Our emphasis, he says, must be on *selection,* not supply, if we are to avoid chaos.

Have you noticed a lot of people carrying around notebooks lately and clutching them as though their lives depended on their contents? These individuals see the problem and are implementing their own "selection" tool for handling their personal information overload. The scores of "organizers" proliferating in retail stores and mail-order markets are not a passing popularity item. They are essential to our effectiveness in the information age.

What trips most of us up is losing details through proverbial cracks in the floor. When you have a system for managing the particulars, you won't miss meetings, lose directions, or forget to place that important phone call. Such details, when mislaid, can cost you dearly. I know people who have lost promising clients just because they failed to follow through on a simple, but significant, matter.

The Notebook Consolidation System

In order to cope with the information explosion, you must clarify and consolidate the data you need to competently conduct your business and personal affairs. You can do this by setting up a compact loose-leaf notebook to serve as a clearing house for all you do. An effective organizing tool integrates all the information vital to your functioning and facilitates a flow in your life. It should have sections for the following:

Monthly calendars—for long-range planning (trips, projects, events) and important reminders (birthdays and anniversaries, special sales, etc.)

Weekly schedules—for commitments that reflect your goals and priorities

Agendas—for ongoing communications with key people and for items to be dealt with at regular meetings

Goals—to keep the whole picture of your life fresh and progressing

Projects—for mind maps and related information (*see* chapter 11)

To dos—for specific tasks that are not part of a project (phone calls, correspondence, reminder to pick up cleaning, etc.)

Daily planner—to organize your *A* and *B* priorities (which you transfer daily from the above sections)

Notes—for note taking, keeping lists

Finances—for keeping track of budgets, expenditures, and receipts

Addresses—for frequently used addresses and phone numbers

Never keep separate calendars at home and at work, or you will commit management suicide. Remember, we are talking about *life* management; so your personal and professional planning should be contained in the same system.

Since this system will go just about everywhere with you,

choose something you will enjoy using. You will "wear" it more than any other accessory in your wardrobe, so don't skimp. No price is too high for personal organization. It will pay for itself in time saved, within weeks. Buy a good retractable pencil while you're at it. Don't use a pen on your schedule.

If you want a ready-made organizer, I can recommend *The Personal Resource System,** which is what I use. Some of its benefits are:

1. *Simplicity.* It is uncomplicated and easy to use, but it is thorough in covering all the bases.

2. *Organization and clarity.* Everything you need to manage life on a daily basis is in one place (you can say good-bye to yellow stickers that decorate your desk and refrigerator), and each section reinforces the others.

3. *Instant accessibility.* You know exactly where to record or retrieve information, as opposed to searching for something you wrote down but cannot remember where.

4. *Maintaining the overview.* It is based on a methodology that incorporates the whole philosophy of life management espoused in this book.

5. *Reinforcing good habits.* When used as designed, it consistently produces positive results.

6. *Flexibility.* It adapts fully to your own needs and management style.

7. *Training.* The system comes with a cassette tape and an illustrated guide that instruct you in its implementation.

People often ask me, "Doesn't it take work to use the kind of system you're talking about?" Of course it does! It takes work to be organized. But, remember, it takes *more* work to be *disorganized*!

The personnel director of a well-known corporation had the same objection, and suggested that it would require too much time to record all that information. I asked him in return: "Which is the better option: to take two seconds to write down

* For more information, write to: Personal Resource System, P.O. Box 45777, Seattle, WA 98145.

the flight number and arrival time of a friend's plane where you know you can locate it, or to take twenty minutes to rummage through the wastebasket to find the piece of paper you put it on?" He grinned sheepishly, because (unbeknown to me at the time) the reason he kept me waiting for our appointment is that he had spent thirty minutes looking through the wastebasket for an order number he had lost. He set up an organizer that afternoon.

If you don't like the idea of writing everything in a notebook, consider that you are already writing it somewhere; but without a central system, you usually forget where. Most details necessary to managing yourself take seconds to record and retrieve in a well-organized notebook. But they take minutes and maybe hours to locate when left loose in drawers, on counters or desks, at the phone, or who knows where. Picture yourself going to one place for a vital bit of information and knowing it will be there, instead of running around the house or office looking for it on your way out the door to a store or meeting.

Recently, computer software has been produced to replace a notebook organizer. Personally, I don't believe it could ever accomplish in effectiveness or efficiency what your own, in-hand system can do. The few users I have talked to agree that it takes more time to call up something as simple as a scheduled appointment, let alone change it, than to just flip to your own calendar pages with a pencil and eraser. Further, you can't carry it to a powder room or pay phone; and, most importantly, you miss the whole picture.

Whatever system you use, keep it current. As you complete projects, for example, transfer those pages to another notebook for easy referral later on. Don't accumulate information you are no longer using or material that is too cumbersome to carry around. For instance, if you are redecorating your home, you will keep working information in your system: your overall plan; names and phone numbers of furniture and fabric stores; measurements, and so on. But what will you do with catalogues, clippings, and other paraphernalia?

The Companion Filing System

Companion to a notebook organizer is a filing system. Files vary widely, from cardboard, plastic, and metal boxes you can find at variety stores, to sturdy steel cabinets sold at office suppliers. Look over the selection and talk to sales people before you buy. Also check the sale ads for markdowns. If you will be using your file every day, it pays to invest in a high-grade suspension model.

The letter-size, rather than the legal-size, file is standard and the best for home use. Purchase a box of manila folders, and buy labels in a few different colors to distinguish clearly between major divisions. If you have a cabinet, you can subdivide subjects further by using Pendaflex hanging folders, which in turn can hold several manila folders.

Following is one example of how to set up a personal filing system.

General Administration

Tickler—43 folders, one for each day and month, for planning ahead and following through*

Projects—to correspond with the project pages in your organizer

To do—to correspond with "To do" pages in your organizer

To file—for holding papers until you can sort and file them (Before you put them in this folder, determine which file they will go in and write that title on the papers so you don't have to reread them all over again.)

---

* Example 1: Suppose you receive a notice in January of your high school reunion to be held in August. The letter says you must respond by May 10. You put all the information in the folder marked May. On April 30 you transfer everything in your May folder to the appropriately numbered daily folders, so the reunion material goes in folder number 10 (or sooner). After you send your RSVP, you receive a map to the reunion location and other details. These go in your August file.

Example 2: If you send a lot of greeting cards, buy or make them at least one month in advance, address, and put them in your tickler file. You'll never again send a belated card (unless you forget to look in your file!).

Automobile
  Insurance statements
  Service records
Correspondence—a supplement to your address book
  Address lists—for membership rosters of committees,
    organizations, and so forth
  Alphabetized folders—to keep copies of important let-
    ters, to temporarily hold clippings and information to
    send people
  Mail order—catalogues, order forms, ads unrelated to a
    particular project
Household
  Improvements
  Insurance
  Instructions—fabric-care tags, do-it-yourself directions
  Mortgage or lease papers
Medical
  Insurance forms and policies
  Records and histories
  Statements
Receipts (if you don't collect them in your organizer)—
  Drop them in as soon as you return from shopping;
    keep a separate receipt file for Christmas shopping
Warranties

Finances

Alphabetize by title of institution or by function.
For example:

AT&T stock
Arrowhead Pacific Bank—Business account
Arrowhead Pacific Bank—Money Market
Credit Union
Credit history
Financial planning
First Interstate Checking
Home Savings

IRA
Life Insurance
MasterCard
Saks Charge
Social Security
Taxes
Utilities
(Check with the IRS, or your accountant, concerning
    what financial records you should keep, and transfer
    those each year to a storage file or box.)

Personal

These are as wide and varied as your individual interests.
For example:
Entertaining—individual files with ideas for showers,
    birthdays, favors and decorations, games, table set-
    tings
Fitness—nutrition, exercise
Hobbies
Holidays
Resumés and other vocational material
Travel/recreation—places you've been; places you want to
    go; things to do locally; restaurants.

These are just some of many ways you might file your basic
paperwork. For example, I showed "Insurance" as a subhead-
ing under each of the main headings for "Automobile,"
"Household," and "Medical." You may prefer to make "Insurance" the main heading and subtitle the other three. Also, as
your concentrations change, some topics will obsolesce while
others expand. (Remember that candle-making folder I tossed?
At the same time I had a sparse folder labeled "Time Management." Now that subject fills two whole file drawers.)
    However simple or complex your setup, it doesn't have to be
sophisticated and serious. I keep a frivolous section in one of
my files for "Trivia." Three of these folders are:

Encouragement—for special cards and notes from friends.
When I periodically clean out my files, I throw some
away, and the ones I want to save go into a storage
box. If I have one of those nobody-loves-me-guess-
I'll-eat-some-worms days, I get out the box and give
myself a pep talk.

Posterity—for those rare relics I could never replace, like
the large, lopsided heart a fourth grader designed for
my valentine, and on which she printed in huge, un-
even letters: "Mis Stanton's all hart—and no fat."

Humor—for the cartoons, comic strips, and witty publications I use for illustrations, send to friends or save for
parties.

Stephanie Winston, organizing specialist, says, "An effective
filing system should: (1) group information into clear and simple categories that reflect your concerns; (2) permit retrieval of
any paper within three minutes or less; (3) facilitate the orderly
incorporation of new files; and (4) provide a simple, consistent
method for clearing out obsolete files."[1] The clue for cate-
gorizing, she says, is to ask the *reason* for the file; ask what the
file is about. Then determine the broadest category. Refer to
her book *The Organized Executive* and her chapter on "The
Fine Art of Filing" if your needs require a complex system.

As with your notebook, keep your files current by regularly
eliminating what you no longer need or want. If you outgrow a
file, purge it before you buy a new one. You may have enough
unnecessary material to make way for the overflow.

For the remainder of this chapter, we will look at three common concerns that have a lot to do with your effectiveness *and*
efficiency: correspondence, the telephone, and clothes.

Correspondence

When you open letters, do you leave them in a pile with
other papers and then fumble to find them later? Do you tend
to read correspondence over and over while the stack on your
desk gets higher and higher? A love letter that bears repeated

readings is one thing, but much of the daily debris from solicitors doesn't deserve your time.

Whether you receive two or twenty pieces of mail every day, you should have a place and a plan for handling it at once. Organizational experts agree that you can do only one of three things with a piece of mail—or any other paperwork, for that matter: toss it, file it, or act on it. Your wastebasket and "to file" folder serve the first two. The remainder are those items that require a response from you—to write a reply, make a phone call, check on a detail, and so forth.

When you first open a letter, read it with a colored pen or pencil in hand and underline information pertinent to your response. That saves reading it all over again when you act on it, which means saving time. What you can't immediately handle put in a special spot, such as a desk tray or a "to do" file. Schedule a time every day or week—depending on how much mail you have—to work through your "to dos." Or, set a target of writing so many notes or letters a day, and squeeze them in during snatches of free time. If you are often in situations away from home where you end up waiting for others (like a doctor's appointment), keep some correspondence handy to take with you. I use a small straw satchel that has a zippered closing and three compartments, where I put unanswered letters, stamps, and stationery. It is easy to grab if I am going out of town or think I may be tied up somewhere locally.

Keep a supply of prestamped postcards you can purchase at the post office to use for quick replies and requests. By using a postcard you can accomplish a lot that you are apt to put off because you don't have time to write a regular letter or you can't find a stamp or a decent piece of stationery: everything from an inquiry to a mail order company to a personal note that saves impulsive long-distance phone calls. Often a short "thinking of you" card is just enough to lift the spirits of a far-away friend.

Simplify letter writing by standardizing your stationery and note cards. Design your own and have a printer produce it for you, or order personalized paper and envelopes from a stationer. This saves sorting through odd pieces in your desk and trying to decide what to write on, not to mention the clutter it clears away.

Keep track of your correspondence on a separate "to do" page in your notebook organizer. Note when you receive a letter, from whom, and when you answer it.

Because of the transiency of our age, people move a lot—and mess up your address book! Use an address system you can easily update and expand, such as the loose-leaf or the Roladex type. Both have separate forms for each name, and various colors are available if you want to distinguish between different groups of addressees. You can accommodate changes of address and add new acquaintances, and still maintain tidy, alphabetized entries. Another advantage of the individual forms is that you can include helpful information on the back side—directions to the person's house, children's names, for example.

Don't view correspondence as a task to finish. As soon as you think you are "caught up," three letters will arrive and then you are likely to feel behind all over again (and not even enjoy hearing from a friend). Instead, look at it as one of those ongoing activities to stay in stride with. A little organization will keep it from feeling burdensome.

Telephone

Erma Bombeck says that if she had to choose between having another child and another phone, she'd take a new baby, hands down! The telephone is one of our modern ironies: It was made for our convenience, yet it ranks up there among our greatest *in*conveniences. The amazing thing about the telephone is that such a small, inanimate instrument can wield such incredible power over grown-up people. A writer told of a Swiss friend visiting in the States who remarked, "Wherever I go, no matter how important a conversation, an activity, a meeting, or a peaceful dinner gathering, Americans willingly let the telephone interrupt whatever they are doing. It is as if they think God is calling!"[2]

Most people are not aware of how much their phone controls them or the amount of time they spend on it. "Oh, just a few minutes each day," they estimate. Yet if they were to keep a log of the actual minutes they gab, it might amount to hours. Very often the woman who can't keep to her schedule or accomplish her priorities hasn't taken into account how much the phone interrupts her and gets her off track. How many times have you been late for an appointment because the phone rang just as you were leaving? Or how often have you been sidetracked from an important project because you couldn't resist the demanding ring?

If you are bullied by your phone, here are some things you can do to alleviate the problem:

1. Unplug it.

This is better than taking it off the hook—prolonged busy signals annoy callers, and they also tie up the city's phone lines. If you have an older phone that doesn't have a jack, learn to let it ring. Or, buy an answering machine. You will have to get over the feeling that this is rude. A recording is less frustrating to callers than a busy signal or no answer at all. It saves them the time and trouble of calling back; they can leave a message and forget about it. Needless to say, if you work at home or operate a business from your home, an answering device is almost a necessity.

You don't hurt anyone by being unavailable a few hours each day. If you were out shopping you wouldn't feel guilty about not answering your phone. So why be a prisoner in your own home?

Don't overdo this and be inaccessible most of the day, like an overly structured woman I know who alienates her friends because they can never reach her. Rather, set aside that precious hour or hours when you can give full concentration to a task, and determine not to give in to that insistent ring.

Try to shun the phone during your main mealtimes. Jumping up from the table not only disrupts continuity of conversation, it also disrupts your digestion. It is very important that you relax when you eat, or your body won't properly assimilate the food. Poor digestion creates stress and functional disorders.

If any family time should be guarded and kept calm—for physical and emotional well-being—it should be when you eat together. You are also saying something to your family and guests about their importance if you don't give in to constant interruptions. Disengage your phone even if you eat alone, to have a quiet dinner interlude after a busy day.

2. Schedule your phone time.

Set aside a period, or periods, each day to do the bulk of your phoning. You will accomplish the purposes of your calls more efficiently—*and* more effectively do your other work.

Not only can you control when you make calls, but you can say something about when you will receive them. Obviously, you always want to be sensitive to people with immediate, important needs. Most calls, however, are not of that nature and can wait. If someone calls you at an inopportune time, graciously acknowledge him or her, simply say that it's an awkward time ("I'm in the middle of . . ."), and ask if you can call back at a particular time—then do it. Often they will say, "You don't need to; I just called to say hi." Otherwise, you might ask what is on their minds so you can be thinking about it. Frequently you can take care of it right then, without adding twenty minutes of chitchat.

By scheduling your phone time, you avoid impulsive phoning. When you are in the middle of a task and think of something to tell or ask another person, the temptation is to break your concentration and theirs by calling to relay the thought or question. Instead, write it on an agenda page in your notebook. Then, you know you won't forget it, and you can refer back to it at a more convenient time for both of you. Encourage other people you work closely with to keep an agenda page on you, so they can cover several items during one arranged meeting, rather than interrupt you several times in one day.

3. Develop conversation enders.

How often have you finished your conversation in five minutes and spent the next fifteen trying to say good-bye? You hem and haw and cover the same territory all over again.

Honesty is still the best policy: "I must get back to the vacuuming"; "I've got to leave for an appointment"; "I'm off to the grocery store."

When someone shares deep concerns or problems, you are apt to hang on interminably lest you seem inconsiderate or unsympathetic. By saying something like "Before we hang up, how can I be an encouragement?" or "What can I do to help?" you show you care while also helping to close the conversation. Sometimes just acknowledging the person's plight gives them what they need. After a friend told me at length about a difficult situation, I said, "Boy, I really feel for you; you've got it tough." She said, "Thank you. Thank you very much for that. It helps knowing someone understands." With that I told her I would be praying for her, and we said good-bye.

If you are a sounding board for the neighborhood gossip, try this: "You know, this doesn't concern me, and I really don't feel comfortable hearing it." Or, if a compulsive talker pesters you, tell it like it is: "I just can't talk now." Whatever the situation, you can always be courteous. A short good-bye is only rude if it is done in a rude manner.

A classic phone foible is talking endlessly with someone you are going to see soon after. You call a friend to make a lunch appointment, then proceed to bring each other up-to-date for the next hour. Instead, after you decide when you will get together, why not say, "I'm anxious to hear what you've been up to, and I have a lot to tell you, too. I'll look forward to catching up on Tuesday. See you then."

When you call a friend to get or give information, and that's all you have time for, say so at the outset. "I just have a minute, but I called to . . ." If the call is of a business nature, stick to the subject, recap the information that was conveyed, set a time for a follow-up call or appointment—if either is necessary—then simply say good-bye. Don't drag it out. The other person is probably as anxious to keep it short as you are. If you're not sure your business is done, you might say, "Do we need to cover anything else?" If you don't, that signals both of you that you can hang up.

When you make calls concerning bills or services that must

be corrected, always get the name and extension of the person you talk to, and also write down the day and time. That saves starting all over again if your case is delayed or misplaced—which happens a lot.

4. Use telephone time twice.

Keep projects near the phone that you can pick up when you're engaged in small talk: manicure set, mending, and so forth. If you have a long cord or a cordless phone, you can even do more. If what you are doing is somewhat disruptive, mention it to the person at the other end of the line. I, for one, sometimes smart if I'm trying to be heard over the rattle of dishes. But when a friend calls and initially says, "I've been wanting to say hi, so I thought I'd call while I clean my kitchen," I don't mind—if I have time to talk. If someone calls me while I'm preparing a meal, I say, "I was just fixing dinner. Do you mind if I keep chopping vegetables while we talk?"

5. Practice phone etiquette.

Let people know the best times to call you, and ask them the same. As you show respect for other people's time in this way, they may catch on and return the favor. When you call someone you know who has a full schedule, ask up front, "Is this a good time for you to talk?" People appreciate having the freedom to say, "No, it isn't," and knowing you won't feel offended.

When you talk to someone on the phone, don't switch your conversation to another person without notice. I am amazed at how many people violate this rule of etiquette. I called a high-school friend halfway across the country whom I hadn't talked to for over ten years. When I was in the middle of a sentence, I heard, "Oh, oh, where did it go? I think it rolled behind the couch. Can you find it or should Mommy help you?" Her one-year-old had dropped a grape on the floor and I was left holding the phone—long distance. If your child or husband or roommate or anyone needs you when you are on the phone, give your caller the courtesy of saying, "Excuse me a moment," before you leave the conversation.

Many will disagree with me on this next point of phone manners—including a number of close friends and even family whose toes I am about to step on. A *Los Angeles Times* editorial expresses my sentiments:

> The telephonic demon has lately added a new device. For an additional fee, you can install a service: "call waiting." A little click on the line while you are talking to someone signifies that someone else wants to break in. The intruder has the right of way.... Even long-distance calls are not sacred. . . . Why is the clicker on the line more important than I am? Why does he, she, it have preference? What is wrong with me?[3]

For all the happiness the telephone was intended to bring to our lives, it sure creates a lot of havoc. Your phone is not at fault any more than your refrigerator is responsible for your overeating. The solution lies in *your* taking control. Don't forget that time management is self-management, and this is one area you need to be tough—or you'll have a lot of hang ups!

Wardrobe Planning

Shakespeare said, "The apparel oft proclaims the man." The truth is, the wardrobe oft proclaims a mess! When it comes to clutter, clothing is a prime culprit. Men don't understand how a woman can stand in front of a full closet and moan, "I don't have anything to wear." You probably don't understand it yourself. When you say you don't have anything to wear, what you are really saying is that you don't have anything *appropriate* to wear. And your frustration may be well-grounded.

Let's face it; women spend a lot of time thinking about and shopping for clothes. And though a certain amount of this time might be considered recreation, a large chunk of it qualifies as a frustrating, time-wasting chore. This is why I have included wardrobe planning among my organizational tips.

One of the best things you can do for yourself is to build a functional wardrobe. You don't need to be wealthy, just well planned. And you don't need a lot of clothes, just the right ones. Less is better applies to these possessions as well as any others. You can have more outfits with ten pieces of clothes than some women have with one hundred. The key is buying things that work for you and that work with each other. The principle is "mileage"—getting the most out of a garment. In other words, the sum of the parts is greater than the whole.

This is called "investment buying"—multiplying the use of your apparel, not just accumulating more on your racks. You should be able to look in your closet and at once see workable outfits instead of idle misfits. When you accomplish this, you will no longer run to the store before every new event to find something to wear. You will already have it. And you won't feel frumpy and out of style each new season, because one or two new accessories or additions will update your look and keep you smart.

Complementary Colors

If you haven't had a professional color analysis, that's a good place to start. It's an investment that is sure to simplify your life. If you have a tight clothing budget, it's still worth the expense. In fact, more so, because you can't afford to make mistakes. Even if you have to spend part of your clothes allowance to have your "colors" done, you'll never regret it. It pays for itself in wise buying the first couple of years.

When you have a palette of colors that best complement you, you won't waste time trying on questionable clothes, or waste money buying articles that don't look quite right; and you'll narrow down your makeup, hose, and other accessories to a few shades that go with everything. Some women ask, "Isn't it boring to wear the same colors all the time?" This is one of the try-it-you'll-like-it phenomena. Every woman I know who thought that way, but tries it, finds that she actually enjoys her attire *more* because she has more combinations to work with. Left to the hit-or-miss approach, you're likely to end up with as many misses as hits. Think about the favorites in your closet. Why do you choose to wear those over and over instead of all the "extras" hanging next to them? It's probably because the colors—and style—bring out the best in you, and you feel good in them.

Before you choose a color consultant, find out what her basic approach is. There are many camps of color analysis, but some are more reliable than others. Go to the person who will analyze you *individually,* rather than hand you one of four or five standard packets.

Streamline Your Closet

Before you shop for anything new, streamline your closet. Even when you have established a basic wardrobe, you should do this once a year. Take everything out, and try everything on—everything! Ruthlessly weed out the unwearables—the garments you feel blah or blasé about, the frocks you can't fix or rejuvenate, the items you're saving in case you lose weight, the pieces that are passé but hang there year after year. Get a forthright friend with an eye for style to help you. If some clothes are still serviceable, but not your right colors, you may want to keep them to hold you over until they can be replaced. But don't buy anything new to go with them.

In your closet purge, you may discover brand-new things you've never worn that still have their tags attached. If they're wrong for you, get rid of them. Even after you pare down your apparel and shop more wisely, you will make occasional mistakes. Everyone experiences buyer's remorse now and then. Don't let errors in judgment control you—or your closet. If it's too late to return a misfit, give it away or take it to a resale shop. The bigger mistake is to keep it and to try to make it work by buying more wrong things to spruce it up. If you goofed, admit it and eliminate it.

Friends say to me, "If I do what you're saying, I'll only have three things to wear." Good! That's the best way to start building a wardrobe. You've probably been wearing only those three things anyway, but you've derived some kind of security in keeping the rest—for backup.

Getting Mileage From Your Wardrobe

To get the most mileage out of your clothes, keep four words in mind: *basic, versatile, quality, balance.*

1. Basic

Build on your neutral, solid colors, or tweeds. Save prints and accent colors for blouses and scarves; and generally stay away from plaids. The latter limit you and get tiresome. The "basic" principle applies to style as well as to color. The more classic the suit or dress, the longer it will serve you. You can be chic without being trendy. The idea, say fashion consultants, is to *use* fashion to express *your* style, rather than letting fashion impose choices on you. Develop a look that lasts. And don't buy a fad frock unless you already have a stable wardrobe— *and* money to play with.

2. Versatile

Buy garments you can dress up or down, wear through several seasons, and interchange with one another. Stay with natural fabrics, and you'll have more options. These are the wools, cottons, and blends. The polyester blouses and scarves that look like silk work well and are easier to care for. Mixing pieces is more important than matching—and less boring. For example, a tweed or coarsely textured jacket with a tailored wool skirt is a nice look.

Any time you buy clothes, consider how well they will team with what you already have, or what you plan to get. One or two new pieces may give you six more outfits. Nine basic pieces are generally considered to offer versatility and establish a base from which to build effectively: two skirts, two blouses, two jackets or blazers (or one jacket and a nice cardigan sweater), a pair of slacks, a sweater, and a dress (which goes with one of the jackets). From there you can add extras and experiment with more colors and combinations.

3. Quality

You *do* get what you pay for. Buying better clothes is being both penny-wise and pound-sensible. A woman in front of me at a checkout line of a discount variety store spent a small fortune on eight garments that were impractical and poorly made. They didn't look as if they would survive two washings, let alone a whole season; and not one was adaptable. She most likely considers finer department stores out of her reach. Yet, for the same amount of money, and smart sale buying, she could have purchased two or three really good pieces that would go a lot further. You don't have to wear designer creations to be well attired; but try to acquire garments that are well made and give you value for your investment. They'll fit and feel better, not to mention last longer and offer more flexibility.

4. Balance

Your wardrobe is only part of the picture. How you put it together creates the finished product. I'll never forget a male colleague of mine back in New York commenting one day, "I don't understand it. Diana wears five-hundred-dollar-designer dresses and looks dumpy. Ann makes most of her clothes, yet always looks like a million bucks." The difference was in their total look.

Never go out of your house without first seeing yourself in a full-length mirror. From scarf to shoes, from belt to boots, all the parts should harmonize to present a whole. People should notice *you*, not the pieces you are wearing. Accessories are not only as important as the rest of your attire, they make or break it.

Your clothing budget should take into account appropriate shoes, proper undergarments, jewelry, purse, and other accessories. And here is where the books, fashion magazines, and even store mannequins can help you. Look at how people are well put together. Their assemblage is often understated, but uniformly tasteful. You want to look complete, not cluttered.

So don't overdo the accessories, but don't overlook them either. They should enhance your overall look, not detract from it. The next time you are in a large shopping center, sit for a while and study the shoppers from head to toe as they pass by. You'll learn a lot about what creates a poor or pleasant appearance.

There are also excellent books on the market to help you analyze the look you want and the life you lead, as well as give you pointers for your actual wardrobe building.

Shopping Wisely

Speaking of shopping, here is how to go about it:

Purposefully.   Decide what you need before you go looking, and always take your color chart with you. Don't try anything on that is not in your spectrum—even if it's free! When you shop without a plan, you're apt to buy impulsively and end up with loose ends, more clutter, and a depleted wardrobe budget.

Open-mindedly.   Don't get stuck on one color or style and miss other possibilities. While you don't have to follow fashion, you do have to live with it. And some years may not offer the variety you would like. Be open to suggestions, but don't be coerced into buying what isn't right for you. A representative from a leading cosmetic company nearly insisted I buy their "new and most popular" red lipstick instead of the subtler shade I wore. I said, "I think it's too bright for me," and she responded, "But it's the 'in' look." I nearly gave in, but decided to trust my judgment—and my color chart.

View shopping as a learning experience. Gather ideas and insights as you go. Successful shopping does not always mean buying; sometimes it's going home empty-handed. Don't ever feel pressured to purchase something to make the day worthwhile.

Patiently.   It takes *time* to build a wardrobe—often years. Few people have the resources to go and get it all at once. Relax in the process, and look forward to adding purchases as you are able. You may find that one season a very special belt is all you can afford and maybe all you need to update your main outfit and give you a lift.

Sensibly. Don't get taken in by super sales. A bargain is only a bargain if it is what you need. Be aware that the notorious "special purchase" racks are not necessarily good buys. These items are not markdowns, but are usually mass-produced at lower cost—and less quality—to increase sales. While clearance sales are excellent opportunities to make headway in your wardrobe and save money, it's not always best to wait for them. If you see exactly what you want, you may be smart to pay full price and take it home, rather than expend time and energy to keep looking for a better deal. I've only had to do that a few times, and I didn't regret it.

Sensible shopping is also going when you feel well and look good, because you will make wiser decisions.

Alone! Shopping is a serious task, and you can't concentrate while conversing with someone along the way. If you shop a distance from your home, go with a friend who means business like you do, then separate to do your own looking. You can meet periodically, for lunch or coffee or to ask the other to give an opinion on an outfit. Don't count on clerks to be experts in fashion. Be especially cautious of overflattering saleswomen.

Some department stores offer a free "personal shopper" service. You sit down with a representative, discuss your colors and your preferences, and she gathers garments on a regular basis for you to go in and try on. Obviously the clothes are from that one store, but you are under no obligation to buy. It's a helpful service for busy people who dislike to shop or just don't have the time.

Being Comfortable With Your Appearance

As you begin to get your wardrobe in order, you will discover more time and tranquillity in your life. You'll be surprised at how much concern and effort inappropriate attire once absorbed. Emily Cho writes, "No woman should feel guilty about spending time on herself. Style is not a frivolous or foolish occupation. It's as basic as our human need for self-fulfillment. . . . One should aim to be not clothes-conscious or self-conscious, but, rather, conscious of *self* and how that self is projected."[4]

If you feel comfortable with your appearance, you will carry yourself confidently. When you are pleased with what you see in the mirror each morning, you don't have to entertain a self-conscious thought of how you look the rest of the day.

Suppose you follow the suggestions in the last two chapters for simplifying your life, yet you still feel encumbered? Then you may need to look "behind the eyeballs," as they say, to less visible trappings. This is where we're heading in the next chapter.

18

Relief
From Stress

We've talked about physical clutter. But a different kind of clutter is every bit as debilitating; in fact, more so. This is mental clutter. Another word for it is *stress*.

You can't dismiss stress the way you can do away with unwanted paraphernalia. Trying to manage your time without acknowledging stress is like painting the outside of your house in the rain—self-defeating. Stress is here to stay. But while you will always have stress, stress does not have to have you!

We all know people who seem to lead a charmed life. All outward appearances suggest they are immune to the problems that plague the rest of us. Their washing machine never breaks down—or, if it does, the warranty is still good—they win bingo games at the grocery store; their house sells in a week, while yours is still on the market after four months; they get the first fantastic job they interview for; a winsome widow falls in love with their toddlers and *asks* to baby-sit—for next to nothing. These are the persons who make you wonder if guardian angels have favorites.

I've lived long enough and have listened to enough people that I feel qualified to come to some conclusions. I call them Stanton's Suppositions:

Everyone has problems.
Most people have more problems than they show.
Some people have less problems than they say.
All people have more, or less, problems than someone else.

It does seem that some people get off more easily when it comes to stress. Why, I don't know. But it doesn't help our own predicaments to begrudge them their good fortune. And I also believe that a lot of people who look as though they are spared aren't. They, too, get flat tires, Dear John letters, pneumonia, and bounced checks. But we usually see their calm demeanor, and so we assume they have no difficulties. Truth is, they may have even more than we do. But they have learned how to live with it. They know how to handle stress. These individuals practice three principles basic to stress management. They may not say it in these words, or even be conscious of what they are doing; but they operate this way. First of all, they allow stress. Second, they isolate it. And, third, they deal with it.

Allow Stress

I have a friend who always smiles. People who know her use such adjectives as sweet, kind, loving, and pleasant to describe her. You would, too, if you met her. She is all of these. One evening when we were together, I commented on a difficult experience she had gone through that physically debilitated her. "Do you ever struggle over that?" I asked. She replied, "No. I must not be human, because nothing ever bothers me." The next day she remarked that she had to renew her prescription for medication for her nerves—but she didn't see the connection, or the contradiction. She was raised to put a lid on her emotions and, therefore, to discount stress.

The fact is, we are all human. Therefore, we are all subject to stress. Remember Dr. Peck's declaration that "Life is difficult"? Jesus himself told his disciples, "In this world you *will* have trials." Some people think that if you believe in God, you shouldn't have problems. But stress is no respecter of persons, or religion. Nor is it a reflection on your character. Everyone has it.

Some call stress the common cold of mental health—no one is immune. Stress expert Hans Selye called stress the "spice of life." He said, "I never try to avoid stress, because it is an inescapable part of life. I just try to make it work for me and give me pleasure instead of pain. . . . You see it's not the amount of stress you have, it's how you respond to it. It can either cause you to break down or it can be of great satisfaction."[1] An educational psychologist says stress is neutral and likens it to the tension on a violin string. "If the string is too taut, it snaps; but if it's too slack, it won't make music."[2]

The composer of this line from a popular World War I song—"Pack up your troubles in your old kit bag and smile"—committed suicide when the Second World War destroyed his illusions. You can't gloss over your problems and go on with life any more than you can put a Band-Aid on cancer and call it cured. It will catch up with you eventually—like the beach ball that is pushed under the water only to pop up somewhere else.

Allowing stress is not only honest, it is healthy. In the first place, you can't deal with it if you deny it. Also, owning up to it discharges potential pent-up emotions that only intensify the next stressor that comes along. If you have ever stopped in the middle of a tirade or a tension headache or a crying spell and said, "I am stressed," you probably felt some relief at once. Seeing stress for what it is keeps it from multiplying.

The subject of stress has been at center stage for some time. Given its wide recognition, it is possible to seek it the way one seeks a status symbol. Sound crazy? Believe it or not, some people like to talk about their stress, just as others talk about their operations. So instead of managing it, they magnify it. It's one thing to allow stress; it's quite another to ask for it.

I doubt that anyone reading this has that problem, because persons magnifying stress tend not to want solutions. Their stress is where they get their strokes. But I mention it because the power of suggestion is great. If you are around someone like this long enough, you may end up feeling more stressed than you really are. So be careful about the company you keep!

It isn't enough to allow stress, or even to acknowledge when you're feeling it. In order to intervene before it does its destruction, you must be able to isolate it and deal with it.

Isolate Stress and Deal With It

Stress has become a sophisticated subject. Increasingly, persons who teach stress-management seminars have a Ph.D. or even an M.D. They delve into the scientific intricacies of the body's physiological response to stress, and some even use fancy biofeedback equipment to monitor stress reactions. It's all impressive; but it is also over my head. So I felt quite intimidated the first time I was asked to speak on stress, because I couldn't grasp the medical rendering well enough to give it in a talk. *I'm out of my league,* I thought. But I certainly could identify with feelings of stress; so I went ahead anyway, hoping some in the audience would have a grasp as simple as mine.

Afterward, a professional woman said to me, "My company has sent me to stress-management workshops, and I have left every one of them more stressed because of everything I was supposed to remember. You have helped me relax and given me handles." That convinced me that the bulk of the stress we face is not clinical or complicated. It is common and identifiable. I respect medical research and therapy because many people need such help. I know a young woman who restored her stress-weakened vocal chords through extensive biofeedback. I simply suggest that before you put out a lot of money, you put forth the effort to do what you can without outside help.

Stress comes in two varieties. One is "eustress"—the pleasant type. This is the healthy tension that gets your juices going and spurs you to reach your potential. Then there's "distress"—the unpleasant and destructive kind that pushes you past your limits. Dr. Selye said each person is his own best doctor and must determine his own stress level, or stress quotient as some call it. You can't go by someone else's assessment, because one person's eustress may be another person's distress, and vice versa. But you can be alert to the kinds of things that may be causing your distress. For the remainder of this chapter, we'll look at three major contributors to distress and how you can deal with them. The next time your nerves tense, see if you can isolate one or all of these as the culprit.

1. Straws

In the sixties, two doctors, T. H. Holmes and R. H. Rahe, devised the Social Readjustment Rating Scale that rated forty-three life events according to severity; for example, 100 points for the death of a spouse and 15 points for changes in eating habits. Persons who scored 300 or more points in the same year were said to have a very high chance of stress-induced illness.

Some ten years later a team headed by Richard Lazarus, professor of psychiatry at the University of California at Berkeley, looked at the crisis concept and found that "everyday hassles are a more accurate measure of the stress-illness link than are life's great traumas. . . . the daily insults of life [are] more stressful to people than major crises."[3]

King Solomon said it's the little foxes that spoil the tender vines. Likewise, it's the petty but persistent daily insults of life that take the greatest toll on our minds and bodies. That explains why we sometimes are unaware of our stress until we're in the thick of it. We all know that one little straw didn't really break the camel's back!

Frustration

There are two kinds of straws most likely to appear in your bundle: frustration and indecision. Dr. Selye believed that these are the most harmful psychogenic stressors and maintained that "neither uninhibited successful work nor even final hopeless defeat . . . is as demanding as the destructive effect of unresolved contradictory efforts."[4]

Most frustrations are those aggravations we call "pet peeves"—annoyances that bug us but don't necessarily bother anyone else. I won't even attempt to list the possibilities, because they are as individual as the people reading this, and, further, I don't want to put any ideas in your head! If you think about it awhile, you can probably come up with several things that get your dander up. Then think about how much you put out getting in a huff over them. Do you spend ten dollars worth of energy on a ten-cent gripe?

The best advice I've heard for dealing with trivial straws is to look for the simple solution. A friend of mine successfully demonstrated this principle. She was not an extraordinary housekeeper, but when it came to her towels, she liked them tri-folded, and hanging neatly in place. To her disgruntlement, every time she went into the master bathroom after her husband, the hand towel hung rumpled on the rack and she heaved a stressful sigh. This battle went on for some time, and my friend slowly smoldered.

One afternoon she called me at my office excitedly: "I solved the problem, and I don't know why this didn't occur to me sooner," she exclaimed. She had gone to the hardware store and bought a towel ring to replace the rack. "Towels can hang loosely on a ring and look okay," she said. "Now we're both happy." She later commented that it was scary to think how this one little incident had eaten at her and was driving a wedge into her marriage.

Some frustrations aren't resolved as easily as the towel rack. But they are nonetheless irritating. Worse, they are always there, dependable as Big Ben. Sometimes we get worked up just anticipating the confrontation, even though we know it won't even matter a few hours later. The simple solution for these straws is to adopt an action or attitude *ahead of time* to deflect or defuse the stressor.

Something that miffs me is the line at the supermarket. Not just any line, but the one that's labeled in great big letters, "Twelve items or less; cash only. " I can always count on someone with a full cart and a checkbook charging in front of me. Then I'm doubly irked when the person at the cash register overlooks it. At that point, I can use up two days of adrenaline and cause waves of tidal proportion. And all that's at stake is ten or fifteen minutes of my time.

One day I figured out that if I *expected* trespassers to be in the line and allowed a little time to read a magazine while I waited, it wouldn't bother me. It worked, and I even smiled at the woman ahead of me. After her groceries were rung up, for over $100, she handed me her redemption stamps, saying, "I don't save them."

Donald A. Tubesing, an educational psychologist who teaches stress management, suggests we identify our regular resources, or energizers, that we can use to deal with stressors. His personal list includes: "Physical resources: jogging, pruning the shrubs. Emotional: hugging my kids, paying my wife a compliment. Social: phoning a friend, having a party. Intellectual: reading, listening to music. Spiritual: admiring the beauty of the world around me, spending ten minutes meditating."[5]

Laughter should be on everyone's resource list—it is a great energizer, and one of the best stress relievers. Dr. Tubesing says, "If you can laugh at yourself, it sets you apart from your problem. Then you can tackle it from a new perspective."[6] Most of us take ourselves and others too seriously. The old quip "might as well laugh as cry" is good advice here. If you can find fun in your frustrations and humor in the hassles, you can often prevent stress from getting to you. For example, the next time someone cuts you off in traffic, try grinning and playfully wagging your finger. You'll be amazed at the response . . . *and* the calming effect.

Frustration has another side that deserves mention before we move on. Dr. Tim Johnson, the director of Lay Health Information at Harvard University Medical School, says, "When we feel that we are under stress, we are really talking about moments of frustration when we're not getting satisfaction from our various activities." He is not speaking of pet peeves, but of periods or places of discontent when we feel squelched, stifled, or underchallenged.

Dr. Selye warned against prolonged dissatisfaction: "We must choose what we *really* want to do. . . . Blocking the fulfillment of our natural drives to a great degree for any great length of time can be a very dangerous thing. . . . Of course, we shouldn't be reckless egoists caring nothing about the interests of others."[7]

Few people have 100 percent satisfaction at any one time in their life. Careers, homemaking, parenting, all have their plateaus, dips, and transitions. During those times we stress ourselves more by harboring such thoughts as *It's just not me,* or *There's no way out.* Most of these situations won't last forever. Instead of dwelling on your frustration, offset it with self-satisfying pursuits in other areas. That's why personal goals are so important. And, of course, if you *can* change what is blocking your fulfillment, garner your gumption and do it! Don't wait for the tide to turn in your favor.

Indecision

Now to the straws of *indecision.* Perhaps you've heard of the woman who was asked, "Do you make decisions easily?" She answered, "Well, yes and no." While she doesn't speak for all of us, more women than men are beset by the paralysis of analysis. As we take on more roles, the problem intensifies. It stands to reason that increased responsibilities bring additional decisions. If you were a decision maker before, you will take it in stride. If you weren't, you'll take on more stress.

Women's propensity to indecision has more to do with lack of confidence than an overload of responsibilities. In the mid-seventies, two women with Ph.D.s from Harvard Business School co-authored *The Managerial Woman,* a consolidation of their research on the differences men and women bring to the workplace. They established that women were at a disadvantage because of their earlier "conditioning." One of their significant findings was that men tend to view risk as a potential for loss *or* gain; whereas, "Women see risk as entirely negative. It is loss, danger, injury, ruin, hurt. One avoids it as best one can."[8]

Financial advisor Venita Van Caspel writes, "[People who] avoid making a decision [don't realize] that no decision is a decision . . . indecision is decision—usually against you. Over-caution is as bad, if not worse, than lack of caution. Both should be avoided. Life will always contain an element of chance. Not to win is not a sin. But not to try is a tragedy. There is no reward without risk."[9]

An article on women and decision making presented the solution of viewing decisions as correctable, not perfect: "There is great liberation in dumping the notion that decisions are either permanent successes or permanent failures. Bad decisions can often be turned into good ones, and good ones can be made better."[10]

As with frustrations, we too often spend ten dollars worth of worry on a ten-cent decision. Someone calculated that in 93 percent of decisions it doesn't matter what the decision is—just that one is made. So it seems that the way to deal with indecision is not to become reckless, but to rise to the occasion and take a risk. What have you got to lose—really? Start by practicing decisiveness on inconsequential matters. For example, the next time you go out to eat, be the first person at your table to order.

Every day we encounter forks in the road that require a decision. Major or minor, each diverts us from the flow of functioning if we hesitate too long at the juncture. Van Caspel says, "Making a decision is a privilege. No one can make your decisions for you." She also says that procrastination and indecision are twins. So whether you're hung up over what stock to buy or what soup to serve, invoke the procrastinator's pledge: "Do something now!"

Remember, straws tend to pile up, so you may have to work back a ways to isolate the instigator. If they build to the point of chronic anxiety that you can't put your finger on, and that a good night's sleep or a vacation won't alleviate, consider the possibility of a deeper problem that may benefit from professional help. But before you go that route, give thought to an obvious stressor that tends to elude us because it often comes disguised as frustrations and indecision. That is the environment.

The Environment as a Source of Stress

Environmental factors are the culprits a chemistry professor referred to when he said that stress is the price we pay for living in the twentieth century. It is well established that hyperactivity is often traced to sugar, food additives, toxic substances, and caffeine. Basic food allergies can cause mental confusion and even suicidal tendencies. Noise may also disrupt your equilibrium. Too much din can cause thyroid dysfunction, gastrointestinal upset, and gradual loss of hearing. Even certain colors are said to calm or agitate one's nerves. And if you feel especially tense in a stuffy office or during a dry windstorm, it's not all in your head. Scientists have found that 25 percent of the population are adversely affected by changes in the ratio of atmospheric ions—the electrically charged molecules we don't see in the air. Certain weather conditions alter the balance and overproduce positive ions, which can distress someone with a sensitive system.

These possibilities, and more, should be considered first if you feel depressed or disquieted for no obvious reason. The health section of your bookstore provides a number of helps for avoiding or adjusting to environmental stressors. You can also consult a doctor or holistic practitioner who is equipped to administer tests to determine susceptibility to foreign substances. Some people are allergic to the twentieth century, and you may be one of them!

2. Habit

I have alluded to this a number of times throughout the book, but it deserves special mention here. Some people are hooked on stress. Those who have researched this say that stress addiction is not unlike drug or alcohol addiction. In the case of a driven executive, for example, one actually becomes addicted to his or her own adrenaline. This person, explains Dr. Paul Rosch, the president of the American Institute of Stress, "unconsciously seeks ways to get those little surges."[11] While a minor addiction may give some people helpful boosts, an out-of-control habit can escalate and set up its victim for a heart attack or other serious disease.

Stress addicts are labeled everything from "Type A" to "Hot Reactor." Personally, I think many of them are racehorses who don't take breaks. One of the best antidotes for this habit is to learn to relax. The book *When I Relax I Feel Guilty* points out that most of us apply the work ethic to our leisure activities. It's not surprising, then, that consulting firms exist whose sole service is to advise people on what to do with their free time. Here's a nation abounding in leisure, and picketing for more, yet not benefiting from what we have. We're stuck on automatic pilot, then wonder why we suffer so much stress.

A public speaker related this incident. An organization called to ask him if he had anything on his schedule for a particular date. He looked at his calendar, then told them, "I'm doing nothing that night." "Good," they responded. "Then you can come and speak to us." "No," he came back, "you don't understand. I can't speak to your group then, because I have already planned to do nothing." He said they never did understand.

Dr. Kenneth Greenspan, director of the Laboratory and Center for Stress Related Disorders at Columbia Presbyterian Medical Center in New York City, says that learning to relax is the best way to counter-affect the result of stress. He suggests three questions to ask yourself that reveal how well you're doing:

Am I racing the clock?
Do I spend time alone?
Am I enjoying today?

Hurry is a child of the stress habit. In your mind, trace the past week, and the times you were particularly agitated. How many of those situations did you bring on yourself because you were rushing? Someone said if you kicked the person most responsible for your problems, you wouldn't be able to sit down for a week. I have always wanted to poll insurance claimants, because I have a strong hunch that we would find out that a

good percentage of traffic accidents were caused by hurry—
theirs or someone else's.

Hurry may be a result of poor planning. Now that we've
covered that topic, you may do better in that category. But this
habit may also come from guilt—particularly if you grew up in
a home where "doing" was valued. You may still be perform-
ing by packing every minute. And this brings us to a third
stressor.

3. Expectations

If you take the first letter of each of our three stressors—
straws, habit, and expectations, you have an acronym that
spells SHE. This came about by accident one time when I
spoke on stress. But it immediately struck me as appropriate,
especially to this last category. The pressure of expectations
may be the greatest cause of stress to the Twenty-Five Hour
Woman. And it probably affects women more than men.

Until now, the predominant ulcer population has been the
young adult male. However, a professor of medicine warns,
"The fastest rising group of ulcer patients is the female population."[12] I think this has a direct correlation to the issue I addressed earlier—knowing your limitations.

Clinical psychologist Harriet Braiker has coined a concept of
stress unique to women that she labels Type E behavior. She
arrived at her theory while exploring an explanation for why
the common Type A profile "seemed to miss the essence of
what was bothering me and many of my female friends and
colleagues." She writes,

> The classic embodiment [of Type A behavior] is the
> tough, successful, antacid-chomping male executive
> with a single-minded focus on getting to the top and
> staying there.... Instead of single-minded, one-dimen-
> sional Type A behavior, the women I knew seemed
> stretched too thin—pulled in multiple, often conflicting,
> directions by what they saw as competing demands in-
> side and outside the workplace. They performed daz-

zling juggling feats. But behind the dazzle, behind the
multi-faceted competence and ostensible strength, you
could sense the vulnerability. They were trying to be all
things to all people. You could almost hear the stress
bombs ticking away. . . .

My clinical observations show that many women
under high stress cope not by being single-minded like
Type A's, but by pushing themselves to be Everything to
Everybody. This kind of woman is not a Type A—she's
a Type E. And the cost to her physical and mental
health can be enormous. . . . The solution does not lie in
forfeiting a rich and complex life. In fact . . . multiple
roles benefit women. . . . But while having it all does not
seem to be the problem, trying to do it all yourself
does."[13]

A female psychiatrist says, "When a woman's expectations
of herself in all of her roles are too high, her energies are
bound to be diffused. . . . Women's expectations [don't] stop
with career, marriage and parenting. I know successful working women who feel they have to be gourmet cooks, talented
seamstresses, tasteful decorators and so on; all of this to prove
to the world that they are truly 'feminine.' "[14]

This kind of pressure we place on ourselves is called all-or-
nothing thinking and, in the words of Dr. David Burns, is a
"script for self-defeat." When I taught school I contended with
unrealistic, overachieving parents. One mother, a high-
powered attorney, was on her daughter's back day and night to
excel in everything. When Jean received a B or C, her mother
called me to say she should get As. When Jean finally slugged
the softball, it should have been a home run. As far as I could
tell, she always did her best. After one of her mother's tirades,
nine-year-old Jean wistfully said to me, "Why can't I just be
average?"

"Dare to be average!" proclaims Dr. Burns.

Does the prospect seem blah and boring? Very well—
I dare you to try it for just one day. Will you accept the
challenge? If you agree, I predict two things will happen.

First, you won't be particularly successful at being "average." Second, in spite of this you will receive substantial satisfaction from what you do. More than usual. And if you try to keep this "averageness" up, I suspect your satisfaction will magnify and turn to joy. . . .

"Perfection" is man's ultimate illusion. It simply doesn't exist in the universe. There is no perfection. It's really the world's greatest con game; it promises riches and delivers misery. The harder you strive for perfection, the worse your disappointment will become because it's only an abstraction, a concept that doesn't fit reality. . . . If you are a perfectionist, you are guaranteed to be a loser in whatever you do.

"Averageness" is another kind of illusion, but it's a benign deception, a useful construct. It's like a slot machine that pays a dollar fifty for every dollar you put in. It makes you rich—on all levels.[15]

Recently I went to a potluck supper for a friend's birthday. I've never met a woman who likes potlucks, and I think it's because it requires so much work for so little return. I almost backed out of this one because I didn't have the time or energy to cook something special. But I decided this friendship was more important than my culinary genius. So I swallowed my pride and steamed a few bunches of broccoli and sprinkled almonds on top. When I got there, I saw another friend brought bread from her favorite bakery, and the hostess ordered a smoked turkey from a deli.

As we feasted on the delicious meal and enjoyed one another's company, we women observed that we were either getting smarter or more secure. There was a time none of us would have shown up with anything less than our most impressive, hardest-to-prepare homemade dish. Instead, since we all had other priorities, we compromised and did the easiest thing. I remember that time as one of my most relaxing social occasions.

A psychologist says that most stress is an "inside job." Whereas we tend to think it's something someone does to us, it's really something we do to ourselves. This stress, she explains, is based on the fear that we aren't good enough.

When you can relax your expectations, you will have relief from stress. Not that all stress will go away, but you will respond differently to it. That's why I prefer to talk of stress relief rather than stress management, because managing stress implies a life of coping, and you're made for better living than that!

19

This Above All:
To Thine Own Self
Be True

Have you heard the parable about the group of animals who decided to start their own school? They thought they should expand their abilities, so their curriculum included swimming, running, climbing, and flying.

The duck, a superb swimmer, was deficient in other areas. So he majored in climbing, running, and flying, much to the detriment of his swimming. Since the rabbit excelled in running, he was advised to attend other classes, and he soon lost much of his famed speed. The squirrel, who was an *A* climber, dropped to a *C* because his instructors devoted their time to trying to teach him to swim and fly. And the eagle was severely disciplined for soaring to the heights instead of learning how to climb.

No one succeeded in this school; everyone failed.

If you have a hard time sticking to your plans, it may be because you aren't being you. One of the oldest institutions on earth is keeping up with the Joneses, and it is also one of the greatest enemies of time management. You defeat discipline when you impose other people's styles and standards on yourself. I have said that discipline must serve a purpose—*your* purpose, not your best friend's or next-door-neighbor's. Going against your grain depletes energy and victimizes your time because you expend efforts in the wrong place.

Successful management depends on a sensible assessment of how you operate and what you can handle. When Shakespeare's Polonius told Laertes to be true to himself, he might have added the sage's precept, "Know thyself." Part of the superwoman syndrome is to ignore inner inklings and try to be something we're not. I'll leave the psychology of that to the experts and, instead, submit three things you should know about yourself in order to effectively embrace discipline and thereby manage your time.

1. Be sensitive to your cycles.

Cycles have to do with the ebb and flow of your moods and energy. We can't always predict when we will feel good or bad, with it or out of it; but sometimes we can anticipate changes, and always we can be sensitive to them as they come about.

A hormonal cycle, such as the monthly menstrual period, is just one of many internal clocks that cause our ups and downs. Research indicates that within both men and women as many as one hundred or more cycles exist, which account for our complex psychological and physiological functions. Fatigue, appetite, mental acuity, sensitivity to pain, and susceptibility to illness are just some signs of invisible influences that govern our equilibrium. Chronobiologists, who study the relationship of time to living organisms, say we are healthier and happier when we don't fight our natural rhythms but live in harmony with them. Sometimes, of course, it is beyond our power to do so, as when we travel and suffer jet lag—which is simply getting out of sync with our natural rhythms.

For the most part, you can keep in sync with your rhythms by keeping in tune with their fluctuations. The smart time manager stays in stride with her system. She respects her energy supply and accommodates it when it changes. You may have days when you are at your best and sense a surge of supernatural vitality. Use those upswings to tackle a tough project or put a dent in a demanding task. But remember that an energy spurt is the exception and not the norm. Otherwise, during that time you are likely to overplan, then later feel guilty because you aren't "living up" to your standard.

We all have those days when we take a nosedive and feel out of sorts. When that happens, don't fight it. When the gas gauge on my car goes down, I stop to refuel. I've also had to learn to do that for myself. Amy Vanderbilt offered good advice on energy downers:

> The Bible tells us that there is a right time for everything. . . . Each one of us has to recognize that there is a wrong time for things too. The wrong time is often when we don't feel like doing something. Anxiety and tension are generated. In this state of physical and mental exhaustion we begin to project what we will do the next day or the next week instead of keeping these plans in abeyance until we have the energy to cope with them. It is an exercise in futility to start a demanding project before you have recovered your energies as a result of completing the last task, although . . . there is such a thing as momentum gained by doing certain work regularly on schedule according to plan. But this system is frequently nonetheless wasteful. Don't force yourself to face a task that can just as well be put off to a more propitious moment. Work done with a dragging spirit and a literally dragging body often needs redoing. It certainly gives less satisfaction than a job faced with readiness and enthusiasm. To bend the axiom, one might say, "Never do today what you feel better about doing tomorrow."[1]

When you feel enervated, consider the cause before you apply a cure. For instance, it just may be your brain, not your body, that needs a break. Many people who sit at a desk all day collapse on the couch after work, thinking they should rest. What they really need is exercise—to wake up inactive muscles and recirculate blood to the brain cells. Everyone should plan regular exercise. And if your job is sedentary, you should also find a place where you can occasionally stretch or walk during the day. Many companies, realizing the benefits of exercise to productivity, are now putting in their own workout rooms, and many people opt to spend their lunch hour there instead of in the cafeteria.

Wherever you spend most of your day, keep a pitcher of pure water nearby. An optimum amount of liquid flushes the system of energy-draining toxins. If you have low blood sugar, plan healthy snacks. The key word in the last sentence is *plan*. If you don't, you'll wait until your pancreas sounds an alarm, then grab the first food in sight—which is apt to be a doughnut and coffee, or chips and coke. Then you'll suffer the yo-yo effect: a fast and short-lived high, followed by a plunging low.

Energy is a marvelous and mysterious phenomenon of the human body. Invest it wisely and the returns will be worthwhile. Respect it, and it will reward you well.

2. Respect your natural pace.

Dr. Hans Selye, the father of stress research, held that we all have a natural pace. Some people he likened to racehorses— fast and vigorous; others are like turtles—slow, but sure. He warned against violating either bent. "The difference is inborn. If you force a turtle to run like a racehorse, it will die; if a racehorse is forced to run no faster than a turtle, it will suffer. . . . Every person has to find his own best stress level, the highest level of activity that is pleasant for him."[2]

Don't buy the idea that faster is better. If you are a turtle, prefer your pace and let it work for you. Remember, it was the tenacious tortoise, not the erratic rabbit, that won the race. You just may accomplish more than your "hare-ied" friends.

If you are a racehorse, don't confuse racing with rushing. A star stallion covers a lot of ground, but always at a graceful gallop, not a jerky gait. Many individuals more closely resemble a roadrunner than a racehorse. This crazy creature actually exists in real life, not only in the animated cartoons. I couldn't believe my eyes the first time I saw a live one. It jetted around just like the one at the movies. Roadrunners are swift, but they are also spasmodic. Whatever your pace—fast, slow, or in between—it should be a steady one.

Each of the characteristics we are considering must be evaluated in light of the others. For example, I thrive on the pace of a racehorse, but I don't have the endurance of one. At one time I tried to slow my pace to conserve my energy, but I felt frustrated because it wasn't me. Now I allow for my swifter nature, but take more rest periods. I've also learned that in some situations I'm a turtle, such as when I pack for a trip. I carefully plan what I will take and methodically organize my suitcase. I have a friend who can leave for a weekend or a month on a moment's notice. She grabs this, that and the other, and presto—she's packed. I decided I should save time and operate her way, so I tried it. It just didn't work for me. I finally relaxed and decided that her speed is right for her, and mine is right for me.

If you do aerobic exercise, you know the importance of maintaining an ideal heart rate during your workout. This is the rate at which your body utilizes oxygen most efficiently and promotes overall health in your tissues and muscles. If your pulse goes below or beyond your proper range, you sacrifice benefits.

Citing jogging as an example, an authority on the subject says, "If you jog too slowly, it may take forever to get the desired effect; if you jog too fast, you just wear yourself out and get nowhere."[3] He explains that two people with different ideal rates should never run together. "One is underexercised, the other is overexercised, and it is inefficient for both of them. . . . *Never again let anyone push you into exercising at his rate*" (emphasis added).[4]

Don't let anyone cause you to compromise your natural pace in life. Whether you are a racehorse or a turtle or a combination, don't fight it; flow with it. You can't measure your ideal pace as simply as you can monitor your exercise pulse. But you can learn where you operate most comfortably and productively, and stay in that range. In other words, stick with the speed that gives *you* the best gas mileage, regardless of what works for others.

3. *Know your capacity.*

If you ran a circus, how many rings would you operate? One? Two? Three? How many rings are you operating now? Your capacity has to do with your limits, and we all have limits. We can only carry on so much at one time. Some situations are difficult because certain responsibilities are unavoidable. The very premise of this book acknowledges the multiplicity of roles demanded of women today. But some of these are self-imposed, and you must take a hard and honest look at what you may have brought on yourself.

Sometimes letting go is harder than hanging on, so you may hang on and stay overcommitted when you don't have to. I have heard from enough women to know that in many cases, the straw that is breaking their back—be it a job, a committee, or a project—is not really necessary, and furthermore does not serve their purpose.

It takes courage to admit poor or passé choices and change the situation. I know, because I've been there, and I felt my very reputation and self-respect were at stake. People *counted* on me; I *couldn't* let anyone down. Then a friend told me, "Sybil, people only expect of you what you give. Keep giving, and they'll keep expecting. Stop being so available, and they'll stop expecting."

She was right. "To be free people," explains Scott Peck, "we must assume total responsibility for ourselves, but in doing so must possess the capacity to reject responsibility that is not truly ours."[5]

A woman with the appearance of a walking time bomb came to a seminar. She looked on the verge of a nervous breakdown, and our conversation confirmed she was close. She hoped the sessions would help her juggle her two jobs better and also alleviate some pressures she faced at home. We talked at length about how she might handle the overload, and I kept coming back to the possibility of reducing it. It was out of the question. Both jobs were her "babies"—one, a home sales business; the other, an adoption agency she started. She was resolute.

After two days together, she broke down and burst into

tears. "I've known for several months that it was time to leave the agency and let my co-worker carry on," she admitted, "but the very thought scared me." She also knew that her work worries accounted for the problems at home, and that they would take care of themselves once she took care of the other.

When I saw her a month later, she still wasn't out of the woods, but she was on her way. The transition would take several more months, and require even more work. That often happens when we get in too deep. But once you plow out, you'll never regret it, and you will be less apt to let the pile get so high again.

If you are in over your head, size up your situation and see if you can eliminate something. If you decide you can, then you must determine how to go about it. Unless the commitment is a minor one, you probably can't just back out of it with a phone call. Treat a major change as you would a goal and lay out your steps. Planning is as important to subtracting a priority as it is to adding one.

Being Yourself

When you put it all together—your cycles, your nature, and your capacity—what do you have? The bionic woman? Probably not, unless your biorhythms are all stuck on optimum, and even then human beings are finite.

Does that disappoint you? It should be a relief. After all, your body has known it all along. Now what will you do with this knowledge of how you operate?

The link between knowing yourself and being true to yourself is *loving* yourself. Dr. Peck reminds us of the crucial connection between self-esteem and successful management: "This feeling of being valuable is a cornerstone of self-discipline because when one considers oneself valuable one will take care of oneself in all ways that are necessary. Self-discipline is self-caring."[6]

The authors of *How to Be Your Own Best Friend* say that if you can't "care for yourself, you can never care properly for others. The Bible says, 'Love they neighbor as thyself, not 'better than' or 'instead of' thyself. If we cannot love ourselves, where will we draw our love for anyone else? . . . If you don't have it, you can't give it."[7]

I heard about a little boy who sadly said to his mother, "Why can't Daddy spend time with us?" His mother explained that Daddy was very busy and couldn't get all his work done at the office. The boy responded, "Then why don't they put him in a slower group?"

If you are in over your head, you just may need to put yourself in another group, and that may be the kindest, most loving thing you can do for yourself.

When you are true to yourself, you follow your natural bent and encourage others to follow theirs. You won't compare yourself to another, or impose your preferences on anyone. The remarkable result of being yourself is that you allow others the same right and the world is all the better for it because energy is more productively channeled. We weren't made in a mold, so we shouldn't put ourselves, or others, there. Life is much more fun and interesting when ducks are ducks and squirrels are squirrels.

Right, Polonius?

Source Notes

Chapter 1

1. Anne Morrow Lindbergh, *Gift From the Sea* (New York: Pantheon, 1955), pp. 27, 56.
2. R. Alec Mackenzie, *The Time Trap* (New York: McGraw-Hill Pubns, 1972), p. 6.
3. Ephesians 5:15, 16 NAS.
4. Pat Means, *Jesus and the Mystics* (Campus Crusade for Christ, 1976), pp. 16, 17.

Chapter 2

1. Cecil Osborne, *The Art of Understanding Yourself* (Grand Rapids: Zondervan, 1967), p. 161.
2. Maurice Wagner, *The Sensation of Being Somebody* (Grand Rapids: Zondervan, 1975), preface.
3. Robert H. Schuller, *Self-Esteem: The New Reformation* (Waco, Tex.: Word Books, 1982), p. 19.
4. Maxwell Maltz, *Psycho-Cybernetics* (Englewood Cliffs, N.J.: Prentice-Hall, 1960), p. 51.
5. "Self-Fulfilling Prophecy in the Classroom," in *International Encyclopedia of Psychiatry, Psychoanalysis and Neurology*, ed. Benjamin G. Wolman, vol. 10 (New York: Van Nostrand Reinhold, 1977), p. 117.
6. Russell A. Jones, *Self-Fulfilling Prophecies: Social, Psychological, and Physiological Effects of Expectancies* (Hillsdale, N.J.: Lawrence Erlbaum Associates, 1977), p. 7.
7. Wagner, *Sensation of Being Somebody*, pp. 28–31.
8. Maxwell Maltz, *Psycho-Cybernetics* (North Hollywood: Wilshire Book Co., 1967), p. viii.
9. Wagner, *Sensation of Being Somebody*, p. 32.

10. Ibid., pp. 33–37.
11. Dorothy Corkille Briggs, *Celebrate Your Self* (New York: Doubleday, 1977), p. 10.
12. Sonya Friedman, *Men Are Just Desserts* (New York: Warner Books, 1983), pp. 128, 129.
13. Briggs, *Celebrate Your Self,* p. 42.
14. Ibid., p. 12.
15. Friedman, *Men Are Just Desserts,* pp. 133, 134.
16. Maltz, *Psycho-Cybernetics,* pp. 39, 40.
17. Joshua Loth Liebman, *Peace of Mind* (New York: Simon & Schuster, 1946), p. 13.
18. C. S. Lewis, *A Grief Observed* (New York: Bantam, 1976), p. 54.
19. William S. Appleton, *Fathers and Daughters* (New York: Doubleday, 1981), p. 120.
20. Allen Wheelis, *How People Change* (New York: Harper & Row, 1973), p.14.
21. Paul Tournier, *The Meaning of Persons* (New York: Harper & Row, 1957), p. 210.

Chapter 3

1. 1 Corinthians 9:26, TLB.
2. *Esquire,* February, 1980.
3. Walter C. Kaiser, Jr., *Ecclesiastes: Total Life* (Chicago: Moody, 1979), p. 41.
4. Ibid., p. 47.
5. Gail Sheehy, *Pathfinders* (New York: Morrow, 1981), p. 264.
6. Ibid., p. 45.
7. Viktor E. Frankl, *Man's Search for Meaning* (Boston: Beacon Press, 1939, 1963), p. 122.
8. William H. Mikesell, *The Power of High Purpose* (Anderson, Ind.: Warner Press, 1961), pp. 35, 113.
9. Sheehy, *Pathfinders,* p. 279.
10. Mikesell, *Power of High Purpose,* p. 79.
11. Frankl, *Man's Search for Meaning,* p. 104.

Chapter 4

1. Anne Morrow Lindbergh, *Gift From the Sea* (New York: Pantheon, 1955), p. 23.
2. Corrie ten Boom, *The Hiding Place* (Old Tappan, N.J.: Chosen/Revell, 1971), p. 15.
3. Edith Schaeffer, *A Way of Seeing* (Old Tappan, N.J.: Revell, 1977), pp. 77–80.
4. Norma Zimmer, *Norma* (Wheaton, Ill.: Tyndale, 1976), pp. 366–68.
5. Philippians 3:13, 14 NAS.
6. Dorothy Corkille Briggs, *Celebrate Your Self* (New York: Doubleday, 1977), pp. 191, 192.
7. Barbara Jordan and Shelby Hearon, *Barbara Jordan: A Self-Portrait* (New York: Doubleday, 1979), preface.
8. *People,* December 10, 1979.
9. Joshua Loth Liebman, *Peace of Mind* (New York: Simon & Schuster, 1946), p. 144.

Chapter 5

1. Walter de la Mare, *The Tall Book of Make-Believe* (New York: Harper and Brothers, 1950), pp. 11, 12.
2. Maxwell Maltz, *Psycho-Cybernetics* (North Hollywood: Wilshire, 1967), pp. 104, 105.
3. *People,* November 28, 1983, p. 90.

Chapter 6

1. Robert F. Mager, *Preparing Instructional Objectives* (Palo Alto, Calif.: Fearon Publishers, 1962), p. 3.
2. Arthur F. Miller and Ralph T. Mattson, *The Truth About You* (Old Tappan, N.J.: Revell, 1977), p. 22.
3. *St. Paul Pioneer Times,* August 5, 1979.
4. *Reader's Digest,* February, 1981, p. 18.

Chapter 7

1. John D. Snider, *I Love Books* (Washington: Review and Herald, 1942), pp. 347, 348.

2. Gladys Hunt, *Honey for a Child's Heart* (Grand Rapids: Zondervan, 1969), p. 47.
3. Ibid., pp. 24, 96, 97.
4. Ione Oliver, "How to Die Younger Later," *San Bernardino* (Calif.) *Sun,* July 13, 1983, p. AA-3.
5. Betty J. Blair, "Holistic Medicine: A New Old Approach to Staying Healthy," *Detroit News,* October 1, 1978, p. 16c.
6. Norman Cousins, *Anatomy of an Illness* (New York: Norton, 1979), p. 55.
7. Paul Tournier, *Fatigue in Modern Society* (Richmond, Va.: John Knox, 1965), p. 8.
8. Dr. Timothy Johnson, syndicated newspaper column, August 4, 1984.
9. Ethel H. Renwick, *Let's Try Real Food* (Grand Rapids: Zondervan, 1976), p. 5.
10. Eugene C. Kennedy, *Believing* (New York: Doubleday, 1974), p. 7.
11. James Fowler, "Stages of Faith," *Psychology Today,* November, 1985, p. 56.
12. Helen Keller, *Let Us Have Faith* (New York: Doubleday, 1950), p. 66.
13. Romans 14:22 NAS.
14. Kennedy, *Believing,* p. 75.
15. Ibid., p. 92.
16. *See* 2 Corinthians 5:14.
17. Alvin Toffler, *Future Shock* (New York: Random House, 1970), p. 87.

Chapter 8

1. Proverbs 15:17 NAS.
2. O. Dean Martin, *Good Marriages Don't Just Happen* (Old Tappan, N.J.: Revell, 1984), pp. 158, 159.
3. "The American Family, Bent—But Not Broken," *U.S. News & World Report,* June 16, 1980, p. 50.
4. Ibid., p. 60.
5. Richard Nelson Bolles, *What Color Is Your Parachute?* (Berkeley, Calif.: Ten Speed Press, 1980), p. 10.

6. Ibid., pp. 42, 43.
7. Sharon Johnson, "Retraining's Come a Long Way, Baby," *New York Times,* October 14, 1984, Section 12, p. 9.
8. *See* 1 Timothy 6:10.
9. Venita Van Caspel, *The Power of Money Dynamics* (Reston, Va.: Reston Publishing Co., 1983), p. xiii.
10. Howard L. Dayton, Jr., *Your Money: Frustration or Freedom?* (Wheaton, Ill.: Tyndale, 1979), p. 28.
11. Van Caspel, *Power of Money Dynamics,* p. 2.
12. Jacqueline C. Warsaw, "The 5-Year Career Plan: What's in It for You," *Working Woman,* July, 1978, pp. 49, 50.
13. Amy Vanderbilt, *Organize Your Life* (New York: Doubleday, 1966), pp. 6, 7.
14. Anne Morrow Lindbergh, *Gift From the Sea* (New York: Pantheon, 1955), p. 56.
15. Walter E. O'Donnell, M.D., "How to Increase Your Inner Energy," *Reader's Digest,* March, 1977, p. 84.
16. Mildred Newman and Bernard Berkowitz, *How to Be Your Own Best Friend* (New York: Ballantine, 1971), p. 35.

Chapter 10

1. Merrill E. Douglass and Philip H. Goodwin, *Successful Time Management for Hospital Administrators* (New York: American Management Association, 1980), p. 6.
2. M. Scott Peck, M.D., *The Road Less Traveled* (New York: Simon & Schuster, 1978), pp. 40, 41.
3. R. Alec Mackenzie, *The Time Trap* (New York: McGraw-Hill Pubns., 1972), p. 38.
4. Alan Lakein, "How to Get Control of Your Time and Your Life," *New York,* January 17, 1972.
5. Charles E. Hummel, *Tyranny of the Urgent* (Downers Grove, Ill.: Inter-Varsity Christian Fellowship, 1967), p. 5.
6. David D. Burns, M.D., *Feeling Good* (New York: Morrow, 1980), p. 82.

Chapter 11

1. Merrill E. Douglass and Larry D. Baker, *The Time Management Profile* (Minneapolis: Performax Systems International, 1984), p. 10.
2. Luke 14:28–30 NAS.

Chapter 12

1. R. Alec Mackenzie, *The Time Trap* (New York: McGraw-Hill Pubns, 1972), pp. 38, 39.
2. A. Victor Segno, *Thought Vibrations* (North Hollywood: Newcastle Pub., 1973), pp. 66, 67.
3. Roger Barnes, *A Guide to Successful Time Management for the Data Processing Professional* (Seattle: Dynabyte Books, 1983), p. 145.
4. Ibid., p. 146.
5. Alan Lakein, *How to Get Control of Your Time and Your Life* (New York: New American Library, 1973), p. 96.
6. Edwin C. Bliss, *Getting Things Done* (New York: Bantam, 1976), p. 156.
7. Ibid., pp. 156, 157.

Chapter 14

1. Amy Vanderbilt, *Organize Your Life* (New York: Doubleday, 1966), pp. 32, 33.

Chapter 15

1. A. Victor Segno, *Thought Vibrations* (North Hollywood: Newcastle Pub., 1973), pp. 32, 62, 63.
2. M. Scott Peck, M.D., *The Road Less Traveled* (New York: Simon & Schuster, 1978), p. 15.
3. Ibid., p. 19.
4. Ibid., p. 64.
5. Richard Shelley Taylor, *The Disciplined Life* (Kansas City, Mo.: Beacon Hill, 1962), p. 27.

6. Ted W. Engstrom and Edward R. Dayton, *The Art of Management for Christian Leaders* (Waco, Tex.: Word Books, 1976), p. 212.
7. John Diamond, M.D., *Behavioral Kinesiology* (New York: Harper & Row, 1979), p. 45.
8. Taylor, *Disciplined Life,* pp. 18, 20.
9. Mort Crim, *One Moment Please,* V. 103/#2, "It's Not All Fun."
10. David D. Burns, M.D., *Feeling Good* (New York: Morrow, 1980), pp. 113–115.
11. Viktor Frankl, *Man's Search for Meaning* (Boston: Beacon Press, 1939, 1963), p. 210.
12. Segno, *Thought Vibrations,* p. 64.

Chapter 16

1. Bruce Larson, *There's a Lot More to Health Than Not Being Sick* (Waco, Tex.: Word Books, 1981), p. 132.

Chapter 17

1. Stephanie Winston, *The Organized Executive* (New York: Norton, 1983), p. 84.
2. Gladys Hunt, *Honey for a Child's Heart* (Grand Rapids: Zondervan, 1969), p. 25.
3. Hilda Marton, "Sorry, I Have a 'Call Waiting,' " *Los Angeles Times,* August 14, 1985.
4. Emily Cho, *Looking Terrific* (New York: G. P. Putnam's Sons, 1978), pp. 16, 33.

Chapter 18

1. Joan Wixen, "Lesson in Living," *Modern Maturity,* October–November, 1978, pp. 8, 9.
2. Jennifer Bolch, "How to Manage Stress," *Reader's Digest,* July, 1980, p. 82.
3. Norma Peterson, "Stress," *Working Woman,* August, 1983, p. 67.

4. Wixen, "Lesson in Living," p. 8.
5. Bolch, "How to Manage Stress," p. 84.
6. Ibid.
7. Wixen, "Lesson in Living," p. 10.
8. Margaret Hennig and Anne Jardim, *The Managerial Woman* (New York: Doubleday, Anchor, 1976), p. 27.
9. Venita Van Caspel, *The Power of Money Dynamics* (Reston, Va.: Reston Publishing Co., 1983), pp. 12, 13.
10. Patricia O'Toole, "Decision-Making: What Really Works," *Vogue*, October, 1983, p. 374.
11. Richard D. Lyons, "Life in the Fast Lane: Can Stress Be Habit Forming?" *San Bernardino* (Calif.) *Sun*, August 10, 1983, p. AA-6.
12. Robert Walker, "Stress and Ulcers," *Total Health*, May, 1983, p. 16.
13. Harriet B. Braiker, "At Last! A New Way to Manage Stress That Really Works for Women," *Working Woman*, August, 1984, pp. 80–82.
14. Elizabeth Howard, "Even Superwomen Get the Blues," *Working Woman*, January, 1980, p. 51.
15. David D. Burns, M.D., *Feeling Good* (New York: Morrow, 1980), pp. 309, 310.

Chapter 19

1. Amy Vanderbilt, *Organize Your Life* (New York: Doubleday, 1966), p. 16.
2. Flora Davis, "How to Live with Stress and Thrive," *Woman's Day*, May 22, 1979, p. 78.
3. Covert Bailey, *Fit or Fat* (Boston: Houghton Mifflin, 1977), p. 23.
4. Ibid., p. 25.
5. M. Scott Peck, M.D., *The Road Less Traveled* (New York: Simon & Schuster, 1978), p. 64.
6. Ibid., p. 24.
7. Mildred Newman and Bernard Berkowitz, *How to Be Your Own Best Friend* (New York: Ballantine, 1971), pp. 35, 36.